CONTINUUM ETHICS

Reasons

ERIC WILAND

D1557530

continuum

Continuum International Publishing Group

The Tower Building   80 Maiden Lane
11 York Road   Suite 704
London SE1 7NX   New York NY 10038

www.continuumbooks.com

British Library Cataloguing-in-Publication Data
A catalogue record for this book is available from the British Library.

ISBN: HB: 978-1-4411-4519-2
PB: 978-1-4411-5308-1

Library of Congress Cataloging-in-Publication Data
Wiland, Eric.
   Reasons / Eric Wiland.
     p. cm. – (Continuum ethics)
   Includes bibliographical references (p.) and index.
   ISBN 978-1-4411-5308-1 (pbk. : alk. paper) – ISBN 978-1-4411-4519-2 (hardcover : alk. paper) – ISBN 978-1-4411-8733-8 (ebook (epub) : alk. paper) – ISBN 978-1-4411-6638-8 (ebook pdf : alk. paper) 1. Ethics. 2. Act (Philosophy) 3. Intention. 4. Reasoning. I. Title.

BJ1031.W435 2011
170'.42–dc23

2011045893

Typeset by Fakenham Prepress Solutions, Fakenham, Norfolk NR21 8NN
Printed and bound in India

Reasons

CONTINUUM ETHICS SERIES

Continuum Ethics is a series of books written to help students explore, engage with and master key topics in contemporary ethics and moral philosophy.

Forthcoming in the series:

Authenticity, Christopher Cowley
Intuitionism, David Kaspar
Moral Motivation, Leonard Kahn
Virtue Ethics, Nafsika Athanassoulis

CONTENTS

PREFACE

You do things for reasons, and it is in some sense good that you do so. You typically know the reasons for which you act, and these reasons are in an important way *yours*. These are some platitudes. A philosophical account of what reasons are should show why these platitudes hold. But it is remarkably difficult to produce such an account.

In this book I try to explain why this is so. I don't presume that the reader already knows much about the literature on reasons for action. And so I hope it is a book that interests and informs both the student and the non-specialist. But I think even other specialists will get something from it, if only by having a richer sense of what the theoretical options are. The last chapter in particular is fairly novel.

There are other books about reasons one could write. One book might focus upon the distinction between objective reasons and subjective reasons. Another might explore the differences between agent-neutral and agent-relative reasons. Still another might closely examine the connections between reasons and rationality or morality. Each of these would be valuable. But I focus upon what reasons themselves are.

I want to thank those who have helped me along the way: Eric Brown, John Brunero, David Hunter, Jon McGinnis, and Mark Schroeder. I also thank my editors at Continuum for their enthusiasm and assistance. I want to acknowledge the generous research support of the Department of Philosophy of the University of Missouri-St Louis, and the Research Board of The University of Missouri. I thank my departmental colleagues for covering my service responsibilities during my research leave. I thank Meshuggah's Café for letting me hang out and write. Most of all, I thank my family for everything they do to make it possible for me to live well.

CHAPTER ONE

What is a reason?

Philosophy and reason

LOOKING JUST AT the etymology of the word "philosophy," you would think that philosophers love wisdom (*sophia*). But while philosophers of the ancient world explicitly pursued wisdom, those of the modern and contemporary worlds have a crush primarily on reason. This is not necessarily a different focus. Foolishness seems to be the opposite of both wisdom and of reasonableness. In the *Republic*, Socrates says that wisdom is the virtue of the rational part of the soul. Aristotle later concurred, and the Stoics thought that to be wise is to follow right reason (or, as it is often expressed, Reason).

But when philosophers now talk about Reason, they usually have something more specific than wisdom in mind. Talk of wisdom, after all, can easily sound grandiose. Today's philosophers are understandably humbler than those of yore. Professors of philosophy don't really think that they are all that much wiser than their colleagues in the other arts and sciences. They know that they are just as likely to act unwisely, as almost any faculty meeting in a philosophy department makes uncomfortably clear.

Philosophers, however, still tend to think of themselves as being particularly good at reasoning, and they even think that they are more rational than most other people. Even if they aren't all that wise, they do hold fast to the self-image of being especially rational animals. Or at least they play plenty of lip service to it. They always have. Here are a few of the best-known philosophical paeans to Reason.

"Reason is immortal, all else mortal."—PYTHAGORAS

"Fortune but seldom interferes with the wise person; his greatest and highest interests have been, are, and will be, directed by reason throughout the course of his life."—EPICURUS

"Reason should direct and appetite obey."—CICERO

"The wise are instructed by reason, average minds by experience, the stupid by necessity and the brute by instinct."—CICERO

"Reason in man is rather like God in the world."—SAINT THOMAS AQUINAS

"All our knowledge begins with sense, proceeds thence to under-standing, and ends with reason, beyond which nothing higher can be discovered in the human mind for elaborating the matter of intuition and subjecting it to the highest unity of thought."—IMMANUEL KANT

"Reason is what makes us us."—CHRISTINE KORSGAARD

About very many things philosophers tend to disagree rather than agree with each other, but their collective reverence for reason is readily apparent. Reason is "immortal," "like God," and it should "direct" and "instruct" us. Reason distinguishes us from the (other) animals. Reason, the philosophers teach, is the best part of us, and we do best when our reason is in charge.

But now one might sensibly worry that all this praise for Reason indicates nothing at all about what Reason actually *is*, but is instead an honorific that a person bestows upon *whatever* she regards highly. Philosophers of all stripes pay homage to Reason, but what each means by "Reason" might depend entirely upon what she admires. I praise what I admire with the term "Reason," and you do the same, but we may not really be praising the same thing. The suspicion, then, is that Reason doesn't actually describe much of anything; instead, it might function mostly as a placeholder for *something* you esteem.

In order to show that Reason is not merely an honorific, and that it indeed has some descriptive content, it is instructive to attend to the views of those who warn us about the dangers of relying on Reason *too much*. We can begin to understand the descriptive content of Reason and its cognates by considering how it is used by those who do *not* wholeheartedly identify with its directive. Then, the descriptive content of the concept—to borrow a phrase of Kant's—shines like a jewel. The idea of what's "reasonable" may be used by someone who understands and perhaps even acknowledges the evaluative point of the concept, without fully endorsing that point. Here are a few non-philosophical examples of odd, though recognizable, uses of the idea of Reason and the reasonable:

> "Reasonable people adapt themselves to the world. Unreasonable people attempt to adapt the world to themselves. All progress, therefore, depends on unreasonable people."—GEORGE BERNARD SHAW

> "A woman in love can't be reasonable—or she probably wouldn't be in love."—MAE WEST

> "Reason is the natural order of truth; but imagination is the organ of meaning."—C S LEWIS

> "Reason is the enemy of faith."—MARTIN LUTHER

> "I tried being reasonable. I didn't like it."—DIRTY HARRY

Here we see various non-philosophers opposing Reason to love, imagination, faith, and even progress. While no doubt some of this opposition is motivated by an animus to some extreme particular conceptions of Reason, rather than to Reason itself, we may still descry the contours of Reason by attending to their complaints. Reason, though debatably important, is not the only important thing. Its significance is more limited that what many philosophers imply. And so Reason is not *merely* some honorific.

Case study: Plato

AS WITH MANY ideas in philosophy, it's smart to return to Plato. In his *Republic*, we learn that Reason (*to logistikon*) is one of three parts of the human mind (*psuchē*), the other two being Spirit and Appetite. Reason's home, we see, is in the realm of the psychological, a view that still reigns. This idea—that Reason is part of who we are—is an important truth that any plausible account of Reason needs to capture. Later we will see that different contemporary philosophers make sense of the idea that you *are* (or your mind *is*) Reason in different ways.

Grant Plato the idea that Reason is in some sense part of the human mind. We still want to know *which* part of the mind Reason is. Labeling Reason as distinct from Spirit and Appetite gestures toward an account of it, but we want to know not only what Reason is *not*, but also what it *is*. Fortunately, Plato tells us that Reason is, among other things, the psychological part that calculates or reckons (*logizomai*) (439d). Reason is the part of our minds that figures things out. There are many different ways to understand the activity of reckoning, calculating, computing, counting, and so on, and eventually we would like to turn toward specifying the activity of Reason more carefully. For now, merely note that Plato here is initially characterizing the part of the mind he calls Reason by telling us what it *does*. Plato doesn't identify Reason merely by saying: "Reason is the best part of us" (for people can easily disagree about which part counts as best), nor by giving us an anatomical account of Reason (as he would if he told us that Reason is the frontal lobe of the brain), but by tying Reason to its activities.

Plato also tells us that Reason "loves wisdom and learning," and it "wants to know the truth" (581b). Reason, thus, is characterized not simply by what it does, but also by what it wants and loves. Reason has its own drives and affections. This can seem mysterious. It can evoke a picture of a little person inside of you who loves and wants things. But this would be a misconception. If Plato is correct, then when *you* want to know the truth about something, it is insofar as *you* are rational that you want that. If you weren't rational, then you wouldn't want to know the truth in question. Reason is the part of you that is responsible for you wanting to learn and know things.[1]

This idea that some *part* of you wants something is intelligible largely because you can be conflicted about what you want. Plato introduces the idea that the human soul comprises various parts precisely in order to account for the fact that you can both want and be averse to the very same thing. Consider: the waiter comes by at the end of your meal to ask you whether you would like to order some bourbon pecan pie. You are a little low on cash, and you want to make sure you have enough money to leave the waiter a healthy tip, so you want to decline his offer of dessert. On the other hand, the waiter's description of the bourbon pecan pie makes it sound so enticing—and you might even feel a bit churlish saying no—so it's also true that you want the dessert. It's an all-too-familiar fact that you can both want and not want the same thing. Sometimes we even *say* "Part of me wants to ____, but part of me doesn't." Recognizing our psychological complexity, Plato decided that the human soul must have multiple parts that want different things. And Reason is the part of us that wants to learn and know the truth, and thus can aim at what's really good for you. Sometimes, we *don't* wholeheartedly want to know the truth: it's all too easy to want to avoid knowing shameful things about ourselves, our loved ones, or our national history; and learning the truth about all kinds of matters is usually not the most amusing or entertaining way to spend our time. So it makes sense to think that only part of you wants to know the truth, and Plato calls this part Reason.

Still, Plato is unusual in characterizing Reason as a part of the mind that *wants* and even *loves* things. All too often, Reason is portrayed as cold and unfeeling; it is usually *contrasted* with desire, passion, and sentiment. So we should think about whether Reason really wants to learn the truth, whether Reason is literally philosophical.

But learning the truth is not the only desire Plato ascribes to Reason. Plato characterizes Reason further in claiming that the Reason-part of you cares about your *entire* self, whereas each other part of you cares about only *it*self, not about the whole "you." And so a person ruled by Reason aims not to make a particular part of herself good, but to make her whole self good and happy (441e). But this naturally prompts the question: just what is the connection between the sort of reasoning that leads one to discover the truth, and the sort of reasoning that leads one to care for one's entire soul? Why think that these two desires go together?

We might be tempted to dismiss this as an idiosyncrasy of Plato, were it not for the fact that almost all philosophers who have since theorized about Reason have also acknowledged that Reason seems to play a role both in acquiring knowledge and in guiding decisions about how to live. These two faces of reason are often identified as 1) *theoretical reason*, in so far as Reason aims to know the truth, and 2) *practical reason*, in so far as Reason guides us to choose and act well. A challenge for philosophers has been to show just how these two roles are indeed aspects of one and the same thing. What unifies these two uses of reason? And are these the *only* two domains in which Reason operates? It seems as though any adequate account of Reason should answer such questions.

 So far, we have seen that in the *Republic* Plato argued that Reason is a) the part of the mind, b) that calculates and reckons, c) that wants to know the truth, and d) and that wants what's best for one's entire self. Much more can be (and has been) said about Plato's views here: I don't intend this to be an extensive account of the *Republic*'s views on our topic. Still, we can register the fact that while each of these four characteristics of Reason Plato proposes can and has been rejected by later philosophers, his conception of Reason has set the agenda for future discussion.

Modern reactions

THIS EXPANSIVE conception of Reason gets radically reined in by many of the early modern philosophers. Thomas Hobbes, for one, held a remarkably narrow view of the nature of Reason. He wrote that

> when man reasoneth, he does nothing else but conceive a sum total, from addition of parcels; or conceive a remainder, from subtraction of one sum from another: which, if it be done by words, is conceiving of the consequence of the names of all the parts, to the name of the whole; or from the names of the whole and one part, to the name of the other part. (1991, ch V.1)

So, for Hobbes, reasoning is simply a sort of mental addition and subtraction. Of course, Hobbes here is using the notions of addition and subtraction quite loosely. When applied to logic and arguments, reasoning involves the "adding together two names to make an affirmation, and two affirmations to make a syllogism, and many syllogisms to make a demonstration." Reason enables us to see how various statements add up—to see, that is, what conclusion they do or do not entail. We are able to reason from some claims to other claims. But reason itself does not provide the initial materials to which we then apply our reason. The initial materials must come from some non-rational source.

One worry about such a conception of Reason can be easily understood by reflecting upon the meaning of the well-known phrase "Garbage In, Garbage Out." This slogan reminds us that even the best computer will generate worthless output if it is programmed with flawed data. The value of what a computer does essentially depends upon the value of its input. While there are ways to program computers to warn users when things are amiss (e.g. division by zero error), the computer is often unable to scrutinize how to repair the information with which it is supplied. If reason were nothing but a way to perform "mindless" calculations upon mental input, then it would be no surprise that many non-philosophers are skeptical about the importance of Reason.

Yet Hobbes goes on to say many things about Reason that seems at odds with the Glorified Calculator View of it. Reason shows us various "Laws of Nature," chief of which is the "precept or general rule ... by which a man is forbidden to do that which is destructive of his life ..." (1991, ch XIV.2). Reason also (or thereby) tells us that we should keep our contracts (1991, ch XV.5), that we should not rebel against the government (1991, ch XV.7), and that a government should be as powerful as possible (1991, ch XX.18). Reason also provides the measure by which people and actions are to be deemed just or unjust (1991, ch XV.10). This is hard to square with the definition of Reason as something that only adds and subtracts! It reminds us instead of Plato's contention that Reason takes care of one's entire self.

We find a similarly puzzling characterization of Reason in the philosophy of David Hume. Hume thought that most other philosophers had overestimated the scope of Reason's domain. Hume is famous for arguing both that Reason determines neither many of our everyday beliefs (e.g. those that rest on the idea of causation) nor our actions. In claiming that "wherever we reason, we must antecedently be possest of clear ideas, which may be the objects of reasoning," Hume appears to endorse the Glorified Calculator View of Reason. And it's true that Hume rejected the then-popular conception of Reason as a faculty that puts us in touch with deep metaphysical or ethical truths. He argued that it's neither unreasonable to prefer the end of the world to scratching your finger, nor to prefer your own total ruin to the slight discomfort of a stranger. He argued that Reason does not motivate us, but is instead the slave of the passions (Hume, 1984a, sec. 2.3.3).

But Hume didn't think that Reason was completely impotent. He held that Reason concerns "the discovery of truth or falsehood"; it is able to judge both matters of fact, and relations of ideas (1984a, sec. 3.1.1). Now Hobbes would likely recognize Hume's claim that Reason judges relations of ideas as just another way of making his own point that Reason is a kind of conceptual calculator. But Hume also sometimes implies that our judgments *about what exists* also involve the use of Reason. Reason "conveys knowledge of truth and falsehood ... discover[ing] objects as they really appear in nature" (1998b, para 246). Here he sounds a bit more like the Stoics. But exactly *how* Reason discovers how things appear in Nature, on Hume's view, remains unclear. For Hume distinguishes Reason from many of the sources of our ideas: from passion, custom, imagination, experience, and perception. And he says that Reason never gives rise to any original idea (1984, sec. 1.3.14). So how Reason discovers how things really are remains a mystery. A positive and specific account of Reason seems missing.

Still, in discussing what is worthy of moral esteem, Hume writes that "Men are superior to beasts principally by the superiority of their reason; and they are the degrees of the same faculty, which set such an infinite difference betwixt one man and another. All the advantages of art are owing to human reason ..." (1984, sec. 3.3.4). Now, it's puzzling why reason should make human beings so estimable and advantaged if reason really were as limited as many of Hume's official pronouncements about Reason would indicate. This has led some to accuse Hume of holding inconsistent views about the nature of Reason (Winters, 1979). Fortunately, our task is not to determine what Hume's most considered view of Reason is. Many elements of his view(s) are picked up by contemporary thinkers, and later we'll dwell quite a bit on what philosophers now call "The Humean Theory of Reasons."

For now, it suffices simply if we register how difficult it seems for even critics of philosophical rationalism to provide a satisfactory account of the nature of Reason. It seems that they want Reason to do things that it cannot do, according to some of the things that they say about its nature. It looks as though Reason has a functional importance to us, and it would be nice to know exactly what it is and what it does, for then we could comply with the prime Socratic directive: know thyself.

Reason and reasons

WE ARE RATIONAL animals; your Reason is a part of you. Talk of Reason with a capital R, however, can easily seem stuffy, pretentious, and grandiose. Let's grant that Reason is probably super-awesome, but let's also temporarily set our reverence for it aside in order to soberly (and reasonably?) assess its nature and powers. Instead of asking the ontologically tinged question "What is Reason?" let's instead consider the more pedestrian question "What is it do something for a reason?" For it's likely that the best avenue to understanding the nature of Reason is to examine how it is you reason. And when you reason, you judge and do things *for reasons.*

While changing our question in this way does bring our gaze back down to earth, it's unclear whether it really offers us the maximally optimal view of our subject matter. Although Reason has traditionally been associated with a part or a power or a faculty of the mind, *a* reason seems to be something else entirely. Suppose your reason for reading this book is that your professor is requiring it. Your reason, then, is not a part or a power or a faculty of your mind. Rather, it's that your professor is requiring you to read it. And *that's* not a part of you.

Having registered this one worry, let's press on and consider further the question: what are reasons? We should not prejudge whether this question has a univocal answer. There might be different types of reasons, in which case a good account of one type might not capture the truth about another. I've already suggested that there are reasons for thinking things, and then there are reasons for doing things. Maybe there are reasons for feeling things, reasons for hoping things, reasons for wanting things, and reasons for many other "psychological" activities. Should we treat all of these in the same sort of way? Or will one account do?

We also talk about reasons in what seem to be non-psychological contexts as well. The reason this bit of salt dissolves in water is that salt is soluble. No mention of minds there. The reason that the mosquitoes are ubiquitous these days is that there's all this standing water about. No mention of minds there either. These reasons are pretty clearly in the world.

In cases like these, when we ask for the reason why some event happened, we are asking for an *explanation*. Explanations seem to answer why-questions. *Why* did the bit of salt dissolve? The answer to the question explains why. The answer also appears to give us the reason it dissolved. And the same is true of the question about the mosquitoes. The fact that there's a lot of standing water around explains why there are so many mosquitoes abuzz. And that's also (part of) the reason why there are so many mosquitoes right now. Thus we are led to think that there is some close connection between reasons, explanations, and answers to why-questions, even in contexts where neither the matters to be explained (*explananda*) nor the matters doing the explaining (*explanantia*) are the least bit psychological.

The sort of reason that explains non-psychological phenomena is thus a reason of one sort. But even it may be related to the psychological too. As we saw, the reason that there are a lot of mosquitoes around is that there's so much standing water in the area, and this reason explains why there are so many mosquitoes. But reasons can also figure into explanations involving psychological stances about this non-psychological content. That I *believe* that there are so many mosquitoes around may seem to be a reason for also *believing* that there's standing water nearby. So when some proposition *p* gives a reason why some other proposition *q* is true, then at least sometimes *q*—or believing that *q*—might be evidence for believing that *p*.

We might question the order of dependence. Initially, the fact that some non-psychological fact can be a reason why some other non-psychological fact is true raises some doubt about the nature of the supposed link between reason and psychology. Perhaps reasons are in the world after all. But *then* we saw that when one fact is a reason why another fact is true, then *believing* in the one fact can be a reason for *believing* the other fact. And there seem to be two options for interpreting the relation between these two reasons.

Here's the first option: the apparent non-psychological link between the two facts—where the one is the "reason" for the other's being true—is just a shadow cast by the *real* reasons that are operative: the reason to *believe* the one fact on the basis of believing the other. That is, perhaps the *explanations* of non-psychological phenomena in terms of other non-psychological phenomena are in some way constructed out of the possibly more fundamental reasons we have to believe things. For example, perhaps we say "The reason that there are so many mosquitoes is that there's all this standing water about" precisely because believing the one fact is a reason to *believe* the other. And so maybe rational explanations of non-psychological phenomena are reifications or shadows of rational explanations of psychological phenomena. If that's indeed correct (although I don't think it is), then we should first get straight on how to understand the latter. Reasons and psychology may be yoked together after all.

The other option is more straightforward, and, honestly, more plausible. We might account for reasons for believing in terms of the operative non-psychological reasons. On this view, the *reason to believe* that there is standing water nearby when you believe that there are so many mosquitoes around is grounded in the fact that nearby standing water is a *reason why* there is a swarm of mosquitoes around. The reason-why, here, is more fundamental than the reason to believe, and the latter is explained or accounted for by the former.

So far, we've considered whether reasons are psychologically grounded, by seeing whether apparently non-psychological reasons should be viewed as mere reflections of reasons to believe, or vice versa. But there are other kinds of reasons to be considered. There is, of course, the sort where one belief is a reason for another belief, as in the mosquitoes/standing-water example. This is an example of what's called theoretical reason. But there also seem to be cases in which the reason why someone is doing something is that he or she is also doing something else. For example, Thomas is reading the instructional manual because he is assembling the bookcases. Or: Eva is checking the patient's pulse rate because she is giving the patient a physical exam. In these two cases, the reason that the agent is doing the first thing (reading the manual, checking the pulse rate) is that he or she is doing the second thing (assembling the bookcases/giving the patient a physical exam.) Neither action is *obviously* psychological, at least not in the way that beliefs are. Actions seem to be in the world in a way that beliefs aren't. (Of course, that it seems that actions and beliefs are radically different in this way could be—and, in fact, I think indeed is—misleading.) So some reason-explanations of actions seem to be a counterexample to the claim that reason is wholly within the domain of the psychological.

Few philosophers, however, are satisfied with this way of understanding how reasons explain action. It is often maintained that the correct way to characterize the reason for which a person is doing something is by mentioning not another action, but what he or she thinks and wants. So—to continue with the earlier examples—the reason (or part of the reason) for which Thomas is reading the instructional manual is that he *wants* to assemble the bookcases, and the reason for which Eva is checking the patient's pulse rate is that she *wants* to give the patient a physical exam. Reasons for action are, despite some appearances, psychological phenomena. And so there's no reason (!) to think that reasons are anything but aspects of our minds.

Whether reasons for actions are indeed psychological attitudes is a question we'll take up at great length in Chapter 2 and beyond. The question whether all reasons are psychological still vexes us today. Plato's problem is our problem.

Reasons for action

REASON, PLATO AND Hume agree, learns what is true. It would seem natural to approach the study of Reason, then, by looking at how *we* reason about what is true. What are the principles of sound reasoning? What counts as a reason to think that something's true? (Or, alternatively, for what reasons *are* things true.)

This, however, is not the approach I will take here. As we've seen, many of the great philosophers have thought that reason has both a practical and a theoretical role. Unreasonable people not only believe foolishly; they also act foolishly. Paragons of reason *live* impressively. It would also be reasonable of us to investigate the practical role of reason.

A second reason for focusing upon the practical role of reason is that actions are the only (or best?) category of thing for which we have a reason that is not itself obviously psychological. Reasons for belief, for example, are reasons for something psychological. The same is true about reasons for emotions and reasons for wanting. But actions aren't obviously psychological; they appear to be events in the world. And if the nature of a reason depends at all upon the category of thing for which it is a reason, then reasons for *action* will be the most interesting sort of reason for us to investigate.

So we will be looking into different substantive views about reasons for action. But before we investigate any of these views, it's important to understand that a sizable minority of philosophers think that any such project is beset with a problem. They hold that there can be no true, interesting account of what a reason is, for any such account will be hopelessly circular.[2] Derek Parfit writes that

> Reasons for acting, we might say, are facts that *count in favour*, of some act. But "counting in favour of" means "giving a reason for". Or we might say that, if we have *most reason* to act in some way, that is what we *ought rationally* to do, or—more colloquially—what we *should* do. But we could not understand this use of "should" unless we had the concept of a reason. (1997, p 121)

Tim Scanlon similarly begins his book by writing:

> I will take the idea of a reason as primitive. Any way of explaining what it is to be a reason for something seems to me to lead back to the same idea: a consideration that counts in favour of it. "Counts in favour how?" one might ask. "By providing a reason for it" seems to be the only answer. (2000, p 17)

Sometimes this point is expressed by saying that reasons aren't *reducible* to other notions. And this point is plausible: it would be very surprising if we could supply necessary and sufficient conditions for the claim that there is a reason for someone to do something. (Although, as we shall see, some *do* indeed try to reduce reasons to other things: psychological states, explanations, and other normative notions.) And what goes for reasons for action also holds for reasons for belief: the Scanlon/Parfit point is about the very concept of a reason.

But even if we can't *reduce* reasons to something else, we still might be able to say *some* general substantive and interesting things about reasons. And of course Parfit and Scanlon themselves go on to make many substantive and interesting claims about reasons in their respective works, as we will see in Chapter 4. It's not as though quietism is the only alternative to a complete reduction. So as we consider various proposals about the nature of reasons, we should attend to the question whether each proposal purports to reduce reasons to something else entirely, to provide only a necessary (or only a sufficient) condition for something to be a reason, or merely to shed light on reasons in some less sweeping but still substantive way. That's what I intend to do.

Overview

HERE IS AN overview of the rest of the book. In the next two chapters, we'll examine the view that reasons are in some way or other psychological attitudes: psychologism. Some argue a reason is a union of a belief and a desire; some maintain that a reason is a belief alone; and some hold that reasons are related to intentions. The idea that we can understand reasons by understanding the mind is exciting. The principal challenge for this view, however, is to capture accurately the sense in which reasons are genuinely normative, that reasons embody a standard that we are criticizable for not meeting. So in Chapter 2, we will examine the proposal that reasons are based specifically upon desires. Then in Chapter 3, we will examine the proposal that reasons are based specifically upon beliefs.

In Chapter 4, we'll consider the rival claim that reasons are not items of the mind at all, but are facts or truths that typically don't depend upon what anyone thinks of them, a claim I'll call factualism. According to factualism, reasons for action are in the world, not in the mind of the agent who has them. If this view is right, then it seems that there is plenty of room to make sense of the idea that people can fail to live up to what reason demands. But the principal challenge for this view is to capture accurately the sense in which reasons for action can motivate the agent who has these reasons.

In Chapter 5, we'll look at some proposals that seek to combine the most plausible features of psychologism with those of factualism. If such a proposal is correct, then there are multiple kinds of reasons. These hybrid theories thus distinguish explanatory or motivating reasons from normative or justificatory reasons. The principal challenge for a hybrid theory is to articulate how these various types of reasons are related to one another in a way that doesn't seem ad hoc.

In Chapter 6, we consider a very different family of theories of reasons for action: constitutivism. Constitutivists think that it's fruitless to offer a theory of reasons for action without first determining what action itself is. The view rests on the thought that reasons for action must be related to the constitutive aim of action; if we can figure out what all actions aim at just in virtue of being actions, then we will be well on our way to figuring out what reasons for action are.

In Chapter 7, we consider a final family of accounts of reasons for action: Anscombean views. According to Anscombeans, reasons for action are themselves *other* actions you are performing. The reason to do one thing is that you are already doing another thing that is furthered by or can incorporate the first action. Anscombean views are less popular among philosophers than the other views I discuss. I don't think this inattention is warranted; while it has its problems, I think that Anscombean views have fewer problems than the other views available. But we have lots of ground to cover before then ...

CHAPTER TWO

Psychologism: desires

Introduction

IN THE MOST influential philosophical work ever written, Plato claimed that Reason is a part of the human psyche. Today, the standard view about reasons for action is that reasons are psychological attitudes. If there is a link between the idea that Reason is a psychological capacity and the idea that reasons are psychological attitudes, perhaps not much has changed.

This chapter has two aims. First, we will look at some of the most important *contemporary* arguments for the claim that reasons for action are psychological in nature. Like others, I will call this claim *psychologism*, and I will sometimes call the defender of psychologism a *psychologist*, although it is important to distinguish this meaning of the term *psychologist* from its typical meaning. The arguments for psychologism are novel, difficult, and impressive. Second, I will assess the cogency of these arguments. I'll tip my hand, and acknowledge that I'll be arguing that reasons are probably not psychological in nature. Or, more precisely, I'll eventually argue that *the way* in which reasons are psychological is very different from the way psychologistic theories typically depict the nature of reasons.

Let's begin with an example. You are now reading this book. For what reason? One likely answer is that you want to learn more about how philosophers understand reasons, and you think that reading this book would help you learn this. Let's examine the form of this answer. It says that 1) you want something, and 2) you believe that doing something is a way of getting what you want. Your reason, then, appears to be (or be related to) a pair of psychological attitudes that fit together in this way.

There are at least two impressive features of this brief analysis of a reason for action. For now, let's just roughly sketch them.

First, if reasons are psychological, then it appears that reasons can *explain* action. Plausibly, that you are now reading this book is explained at least in part by your state of mind. If you had different thoughts or wants, you might not be reading this book. But reading this book makes sense given what you want and what you think. If reasons are psychological, then the reasons themselves explain what you are doing. And an account of reasons should show how reasons do this.

We should be more specific. It's not just that reasons can explain the actions for which they are reasons. All *kinds* of things are potentially explanatory. Reasons aren't unique in this respect. What special about reasons for action is that they explain actions in a distinctive way. Reasons for action motivate action. We do things *for* reasons. They don't just explain what we do, not in the way that our genes explain what we do. Rather, they explain what we do in the sense that we can act *for* reasons. (By way of contrast, we don't act for genes.)

Now psychological attitudes can seem to be the right sort of thing to motivate action. For motivation is a kind of process that only beings with minds undergo. In other words, rocks and trees aren't motivated, this despite the fact that there are also explanations of what they "do." Only creatures with minds are *motivated* to do things. And if reasons motivate action, then it should be no surprise that reasons have to do with the mental.

That's the first basic feature. The second has to do with what we might call alienation. It's reasonable (!) to think that what you have reason to do should speak to you. It should appeal to either your interests, or your desires, or your values, or your convictions. It should appeal to *you*. There's something disheartening about the thought that you have reasons to do things that you in no way care about. It is instead more intuitive to think that the reasons you have are related somehow to the things that are important to you.

Your psychological attitudes seem to be the perfect candidate to capture this idea. If something is important to you, this will be reflected in (or even constituted by) your thoughts. An account of reasons that locates reasons in the mind, then, seems well suited to account for the ways in which you are not alienated from your reasons.

These two features I've characterized only very roughly. There are more subtle reasons for thinking that reasons are psychological. But now let's focus on the thought that reasons might be desire-belief *pairs*, using this idea to test the thought that reasons are psychological in the first place.

Davidson

ANY CONTEMPORARY DISCUSSION of the nature of reasons for action should review Donald Davidson's seminal paper "Actions, Reasons, Causes" (Davidson, 1963). Nearly everything written about reasons for action in the last fifty years owes a debt to Davidson's work, even when explicitly opposed to its main themes. And "Actions, Reasons, Causes" is where Davidson's program began.

This paper starts by asking the question "What is the relation between a reason and an action when the reason explains the action by giving the agent's reason for doing what he did?" Suppose you log in to your computer. And suppose your reason for doing this is to see whether you have received any email from your sister. What is the relation between this action (logging in to your computer) and this reason (to see whether you received any email from your sister)? Davidson proposes the following answer:

> Whenever someone does something for a reason ... he can be characterized as (a) having some sort of pro attitude toward actions of a certain kind, and (b) believing (or knowing, perceiving, noticing, remembering) that his action is of that kind. (p 685)

Here Davidson explicitly associates reasons with psychological attitudes. Look specifically at the first condition. When speaking of a "pro attitude," Davidson means to refer to a wide variety of possible psychological stances, including "desires, wantings, urges, promptings, and a great variety of moral views, aesthetic principles, economic prejudices, social conventions, and public and private goals and values in so far as these can be interpreted as attitudes of an agent directed toward actions of a certain kind" (p 686). Whew! The term "pro attitude" covers a lot of ground. A pro attitude is just *some* sort of favorable attitude toward a certain kind of action. If you have an urge to listen to something dissonant, then you have a pro attitude toward listening to dissonant things. And if I am in favor of defending my country, I have a pro attitude toward *that* kind of action too. Davidson even seems to intend for what Kant called "duty" to fit within the scope of what counts as a pro attitude. Later philosophers invented a technical sense of the word "desire" intended to cover the same sort of range of cases. But there are advantages in retaining Davidson's patently artificial terminology.

The second condition is more straightforward. When you do something for a reason, you *think* that what you do is of a certain sort, the sort towards which you also have a pro attitude. Suppose you attend a Sonic Youth concert for a reason. And suppose that in doing so, you have a pro attitude toward listening to something dissonant, and you believe that attending the Sonic Youth concert would count as listening to something dissonant. Doing something for a reason entails *thinking* something about the act you propose to do—namely, to think that it's in some way favorable.

Now none of this denies that you might think what you do is *also* of a *second* sort towards which you lack a pro attitude, or even toward which you hold a con attitude. A particular action can almost always be categorized in different ways. You might think that attending the Sonic Youth concert, in addition to being of the sort "listening to something dissonant," is also of the sort "bad for your hearing." And you presumably lack any *pro* attitude toward actions that are bad for your hearing. There are drawbacks to almost any favorable action. Life is complex. Doing something for a reason requires only that you think that there is *something* to be said for it, not that there is everything to be said for it, or even that it is best. When you do something for a reason, you think that it is desirable in at least one way. So this is a weak condition, itself comparatively uncontroversial.

But Davidson (1963, p 686) next makes a bolder claim:

> Giving the reason why an agent did something is often a matter of naming the pro attitude (a) or the related belief (b) or both; let me call this pair the *primary reason* why the agent performed the action.

Here Davidson says that the reason why the agent acted often *is* the pair of psychological attitudes she had.[1] In the above example, Davidson would construe your reason for logging on to the computer to be your wanting to check your email and your thought that logging on to the computer would be a way of checking email. But it's one thing to claim that whenever you act for a reason, you must *have* certain psychological attitudes. It is another thing altogether to say that the psychological attitudes that you have *are* themselves the reason why you act. What justifies calling this pair of attitudes the reason itself?

To see, we will need to look at the main arguments of "Actions, Reasons, Causes." Davidson says that he seeks to defend two claims in this paper:

> 1. For us to understand how a reason of any kind rationalizes an action it is necessary and sufficient that we see, at least in essential outline, how to construct a primary reason.

> 2. The primary reason for an action is its cause. (1963, p 686)

The first is a claim about what it takes for us to *understand* how a reason rationalizes an action, not a claim about what a reason itself is. It may be true that understanding an agent's reason is nothing but seeing how to attribute a pair of psychological attitudes to the agent. But this would not establish what reasons themselves are, not unless the metaphysics of reasons depends upon the epistemology of reasons. There's nothing here that establishes that the *agent's* reasons are mind-dependent. So even if Davidson can make good on the first claim, this will not justify calling the pair of psychological attitudes the agent's reason, at least not without some further argument.

But his second claim is more helpful. Suppose that Davidson can argue successfully that the pair of psychological attitudes he focuses upon—the thing Davidson wants to *call* "a reason"—indeed causes the action in question. And suppose we also accept that the agent's reason—whatever *that* turns out to be—causes the same action. Then, we would have strong grounds for thinking that the agent's reason really *is* just the pair of psychological attitudes Davidson draws our attention to. And this would justify Davidson's decision to call this pair of psychological attitudes a reason.

Before we look at Davidson's argument for this claim, it is important to appreciate how intuitive some claim of this sort is. When you act for a reason, the reason explains why you so act. Reasons can motivate the agent whose reasons they are. Any plausible account of reasons should show why this is so. This desideratum of an account of reasons is sometimes called the *Explanatory Constraint* (Dancy, 2003, pp 101, 112–13.) Davidson attempts to show that his account of reasons meets the Explanatory Constraint by arguing that reasons cause action. After all, causal explanation is one form of explanation.

To make good on this claim, Davidson draws attention to the fact that the idea that Agnes acts for a reason entails more than 1) Agnes acts, and 2) Agnes merely *has* a reason for so acting. For she can have a reason to do something, do that very thing, but not do it *for* that reason. She may do it for some other reason altogether.

Let's illustrate. If you go to the Sonic Youth show for the reason that you want to hear some dissonant music, then *your* reason for going might be different from *my* reason for going, even if I too want to hear some dissonant music. Even though I too want to listen to dissonant music, I don't go for *that* reason: suppose that I am going instead for the reason that I hope to meet you at the show. So although I do want what you want, my reason for going is not the same as yours. My reason for going is that I want to meet you (and that I believe that by going to the Sonic Youth show I will meet you). And so I go to the show *because* I want to meet you, and not *because* I want to hear some dissonant music.

So, it appears that we can have multiple reasons for some particular action but act only for one of these reasons. Davidson, impressed by this fact, aims to explain the sense of the "because" in claims like "I am going to the show because I want to meet you." The way to explain this sense of the "because," he argues, is simply that reasons *cause* action. If I go to the show because I want to meet you, then my wanting to meet you, rather than my wanting to hear dissonant music, caused me to go to the show. It is the causal power of reasons that is captured by the "because" in reasons explanations. Call this the *Multiple Reasons Argument*.

The Multiple Reasons Argument attempts to establish that reasons cause action on the grounds that 1) one can have multiple reasons for some action, 2) one can act for only one (or some) of these reasons, 3) the best way to account for the difference between the reasons you do act upon and the reasons you do not act upon is that only the former reasons cause the action in question. Establishing this would then further support the claim that reasons are psychological if we also accept 4) reasons can cause actions only if they are psychological.

Let's evaluate this argument, step by step. First, it is nearly undeniable that one can have multiple reasons for the same action at once. The most plausible way of denying it would be to argue that people act only for *one* sort of reason, say, pleasure. If this were true, then one would never have multiple reasons for action. But this idea certainly runs contrary to ordinary thought and practice. It certainly seems that one can have multiple reasons for action. Don't you have multiple reasons for doing philosophy?

The second claim appears more vulnerable. Is it really true that you can act for one but not another reason that you have? It seems so, but a moment's reflection should reveal that it is not *obviously* true.

Consider the analogous case of belief. Suppose you have two reasons for believing some mathematical claim: 1) you understand the proof for it, and 2) a famous mathematician has told you that the claim is true. And suppose you do believe the claim in question. You could, of course, believe the claim for both reasons. But is it possible to believe the claim for only one of the two reasons, and not the other?[2]

Let's be careful here. If you are *unaware* of one of the two reasons—suppose you forgot what the famous mathematician told you—then, of course, you can believe the claim only for the reason that you understand the proof. That doesn't by itself show that you can believe the claim for only one of the reasons in the case where you *do* grasp both.

We also need to distinguish our question "What is your reason for believing the mathematical claim?" from the question "How did you first come to believe the mathematical claim?" It may be the case that initially you believed the claim for the reason that a famous mathematician told you that the claim is true. Later, you came to understand for yourself how to prove the claim. This does not mean that you now believe the claim only for the reason that the mathematician told you that the claim is true, even though this is how you came to believe it. The reason(s) for which you now believe it need not be identical to the reason(s) that first persuaded you, even when you have believed the claim all along. This can be seen by considering the case where later you learn that the mathematician on whom you had relied was an inveterate liar. As long as you continue to understand the proof, you will believe it for only *this* reason.

We also need to distinguish our question from the question "Would you still believe the claim if you were to grasp only one of the two reasons?" *This* question seeks to determine whether your belief is overdetermined, whether either reason is itself *sufficient* for you to believe the claim. You might regard either of the two reasons as adequate ground for believing the claim, while still believing it for both reasons. Alternatively, you might regard only one of the two reasons (e.g. the proof) as sufficient for believing the claim, the other reason (e.g. the testimony) providing mild but not by itself sufficient support for the claim. But even if that is so, you still believe the claim for both reasons. Regarding a reason as providing insufficient support to believe some claim is not the same thing as not believing the claim for that reason.

So, it's not clear that you really can believe some claim for only one of multiple reasons all of which you have and grasp. For why *would* you believe some claim for only some of the reasons that you see support it? At the very least, it seems irrational to form one's beliefs in ways that ignore some of the reasons you yourself acknowledge as bearing upon it.

I have been raising some trouble for the possibility that you can fully grasp two reasons to believe some claim, but believe it for strictly only one of the two reasons. And I have been doing so in order to raise trouble for the claim that you can fully grasp two reasons to *do* something, but do it for only one of the two reasons. Davidson just seems to assume that it is obvious that you can.

No doubt people sometimes *say* things like: "I went to the Sonic Youth show (because I wanted) to be with you, not (because I wanted) to hear some dissonant music." Let's call this *The Claim*. It is not obvious that the truth of The Claim would establish Davidson's assumption. First off, hearing dissonant music might not even be one of the speaker's reasons in the first place. If so, then this case establishes nothing about whether you can have a reason to act, so act, but not for that reason. The Claim says only that "hearing some dissonant music" isn't a reason for which she went, and this might be simply because "hearing some dissonant music" isn't a reason for her at all. In saying "not to hear some dissonant music," the speaker may simply be denying that this is a reason for her, rather than making any claims about the causal history of the various reasons she *does* have. So, we haven't yet established that an agent can have a reason to V, the agent Vs, but the agent Vs not at all for that reason.

Here is another way to interpret The Claim. In saying what she does, the speaker might mean that although listening to dissonant music is indeed a reason for her to go to the show, this reason, all by itself, wouldn't have been reason *enough* to motivate her. That is, she may be claiming that this reason wasn't alone sufficient to motivate her to go the Sonic Youth show. She may even think that her other reason for going—to be with you—was necessary for her going. But the fact that this other reason was necessary doesn't establish that the first reason played no motivational role whatsoever. A reason can make a difference, even if it is not sufficient to motivate all by itself, especially in light of the fact that people have reasons to do various mutually exclusive things. For instance, she probably also had reasons to do things other than go to the Sonic Youth show, and perhaps her reason to listen to dissonant music wouldn't all by itself have been enough to get her to forego her other options on how to spend her evening. So, the fact that listening to dissonant music wasn't alone reason enough to go doesn't mean that this reason played no motivational role in the case where she does go. And perhaps The Claim indicates only this.

Here is still another possibility. Maybe in making The Claim, she is saying only that hearing dissonant music wasn't the *most important* reason for her going to the show. In saying "I V'd for Reason 1, and not Reason 2," she may simply be drawing attention to the relative importance of these two reasons. But the fact that one reason is more important than another does not entail that the less important reason played *no* motivational role. So if this is the right way to interpret The Claim, then we haven't yet shown that we must conclude that reasons cause actions.

So there are various ways to interpret The Claim, many of which do not support the Davidsonian point that you can V for only some of your reasons for V-ing. But let's not draw conclusions too quickly. Even though there are ways of interpreting The Claim that don't vindicate Davidson's argument, there still may be a legitimate way of interpreting it that does indeed vindicate it.

Here's one idea. Suppose you are heading to the library. One reason for heading there is to read the latest issue of *Philosophical Quarterly*. A second reason for heading there is to chat with your friend who reshelves books. It's possible that you have both reasons for going. But if you read *PQ*, you won't have time to chat with your friend; and if you chat with your friend, you won't have time to read the issue. Now it seems possible that you go to the library for only one of these two reasons, both of which you acknowledging having. In such a case, it would be *irrational* to go for both reasons; at most, you would be sensible to go for the reason that you'll talk to your friend if she is available; but only if not, you'll read PQ. So if you know that your friend is available, then if you go to the library to chat with her, you won't also go to read PQ, even though you think that reading PQ is indeed a reason to go to the library. So this appears to be a case where you can have multiple reasons for performing one action, and yet act for only one of the reasons in question.[3] The Davidsonian interpretation of The Claim seems sensible after all.

Let's, then, turn to the third step in the argument, which is that the right way to account for the difference between the reasons you do act for and the reasons you do not act for is that only the former reasons cause the action in question. This is the step that does the real work. If there is some non-causal way to explain how you can V for only some of the reasons for V-ing, then the argument falls apart. When you act for one reason (and not another), does the first reason *cause* the action for which it is a reason? Does the *because* in "I went to the concert because (I thought) you were going" means *was caused by*?

There seem to be many spheres in which we say "p, because q" and yet we don't think that q literally causes p. Consider:

$(2 + 3) * 5 = 25$, because $2 + 3 = 5$ and $5 * 5 = 25$.

The latter explains why the former is so. Hence, we use "because." But no one thinks that $2 + 3 = 5$ and $5 * 5 = 25$ together *cause* $(2 + 3) * 5 = 25$. The mathematical "because" is not a cause, at least not an efficient cause. Similarly, we say things like "p & q is true, because p is true and q is true." But this sense of "because" is not an efficient cause either.

Here's an example from a different sphere. Jonathan Bennett (1989, p 14) writes that it "seems about right to say that if there is a picnic at z, that is (non-causally) because a group of people socially eat an informal outdoor meal at z." This sounds correct. And it would be at least odd to say that a group of people socially eating an informal outdoor meal at z *causes* a picnic at z. Rather, what we have here is the "because" of constitution.

These various uses of "because" all seem to indicate a type (or types) of causation other than efficient causation. If we would like to reserve the term "cause" for only efficient causation, then we may choose to speak about these other uses of "because" as indicating other types of *explanation* rather than causation proper. We might then say that causal explanation is one form of explanation. The other uses of "because" indicate other types of explanation.

This point bears upon the present argument only if the "because" in The Claim indicates a type of explanation other than causal explanation. If I go to the Sonic Youth show because I want to see you there, rather than because I want to hear dissonant music, does this "because" indicate a causal explanation, or some kind of mathematical or logical explanation, or some constitutive explanation, or some other form of explanation altogether?

Here are some grounds for thinking that the "because" in action explanation does *not* indicate ordinary efficient causal explanation. Suppose Loretta craves a cigarette. And suppose that her craving a cigarette causes her to snap at her sister Tammy. (People get that way sometimes when they are battling addictions.) But Loretta's craving a cigarette is not a reason for her to snap at her sister. Nor was it in any sense *her* reason for snapping at Tammy, if that's even different. It's just that the craving made her cranky enough to speak sharply to her sister. The fact that something causes an action—*this* fact—hardly mean that it really was a *reason* for the action. There is more to being a reason for action than being a cause of that action, even if that cause is of the same metaphysical category as other things that indeed are reasons.

This points to a difference between rational explanation of action and other sorts of explanation of action. The reason why Loretta snaps at Tammy is that she is craving a cigarette (and she is addicted, etc.). But the reason *why* she acts is not the same thing as the reason *for which* she acts; after all, it may be true that she snaps at her sister for *no* reason whatsoever. So not every reason why an agent does something is a reason for which she does it. When we explain why an agent acts as she does by noting that she is tired, hypnotized, depressed, or under a lot of stress, we aren't explaining her action by noting the reasons for which she acts. It is instead a different sort of explanation.

Davidson recognizes that this could be a serious problem for his view. He asks us to imagine the case of *The Nervous Climber*. A mountain climber might want to rid himself of the weight and danger of holding another man by a rope. The climber comes to realize that he could do this by letting go of the rope. This thought (or pair of thoughts) makes the climber nervous ... *so* nervous that he lets go of the rope. The belief/pro-attitude pair thus *causes* the climber to let go of the rope. And, no doubt, a very selfish climber could have released the rope for the reason that the belief/pro-attitude pair stands for. But our nervous climber is not a selfish climber. He lets go of the rope *because* he wants to be safe and believes that he could do so by letting go, but not *for* this reason. His psychological attitudes causally explain why he lets go of the rope, even though they do not give a reason for which he lets go of the rope. So the fact that what Davidson calls a primary reason causes an action does not establish that the agent acted for that reason.

The case of The Nervous Climber illustrates what's known as the problem of deviant causal chains. The climber's belief/pro-attitude pair causes the climber's action, but, Davidson notes, it doesn't cause the action in the *right way*, the way in which reasons normally rationalize the actions that they are reasons for. In other words, the type of causation involved deviates from the kind involved in rationalization. So, *whatever* rationalization is, it is not simply identical to causation. There is more to being a reason for action than being a cause of action.

Note that it is still open to the causalist to maintain that reasons indeed cause actions. The task, then, would be to specify how reasons do that, to explain what distinguishes the deviant from the non-deviant cases. How is the causation different in the case of The Nervous Climber than it is in the case of The Selfish Climber? Unfortunately, no one seems able to say exactly what this way is. There *is* some important difference between the way causation operates in cases of rationalization, and the way it operates in other settings. But we can say little about what difference this is. The darkness is not easily exorcised.

So, this is one outstanding problem for Davidson's view, and indeed for any view that hopes to shed light on the nature of rationalization by relating it to efficient causation. Of course, any plausible account of the nature of reasons should fulfill the Explanatory Constraint. But saying merely that reasons cause action does not really account for just *how* reasons explain the actions for which they are reasons.

Pursuing this line of questioning much further would lead us deep into thorny questions about the nature and varieties of explanation. We are unable here to pursue that very far. We will pick up this issue in the fourth chapter, when we examine the view that reasons are extra-psychological facts. Suffice it for present purposes to say that the argument up until this point supports the conclusion that a reason can—in *some* sense of "explain"—explain action.

As mentioned above, the Multiple Reasons Argument may support the further claim that *reasons* themselves are psychological. But it does so only if psychological entities cause action. We have seen that ordinary discourse vindicates the idea that the psychological indeed causes action, for we say things like "I did it because I wanted to do it." But what grounds are there for thinking that *only* psychological entities can cause action?

This too is a thorny philosophical question we will not be able to disentangle right away. For now, perhaps it's wise just to note that the burden of argument seems to be upon those who deny that only the psychological causes action. Absent a specific alternative, it is sensible to conclude that if reasons cause action, then reasons are psychological in character. (But note that in Chapter 7 we will indeed be exploring a "cause" of action that is not a psychological attitude. So we will see whether the burden of argument can be met.)

If all this goes through, then we have a nice argument that reasons are psychological attitudes. The argument is far from airtight: we've seen that one can sensibly question various steps along the way. But it now should be easy to see why one might think that reasons are indeed psychological.

Psychologism and normativity

SETTING ASIDE THESE difficulties, let us re-examine the more general claim that reasons are psychological attitudes. Perhaps the chief barrier to accepting this straightforward identification has been the natural thought that people don't always have the psychological attitudes that they should, or that people have reason to do things that they don't want to do, or that they don't know about. Reasons are in some sense normative. They justify in some way the actions (or the beliefs) that they are reasons for.

This leads us to see another important desideratum for a theory of reasons: to account for how reasons are normative or justificatory. This is often called the *Normative Constraint* (Dancy, 2003, pp 103–8). As with the Explanatory Constraint, any account of reasons that fails to meet the Normative Constraint is thereby defective. And, as we shall see, it appears to be tremendously difficult to meet both the Explanatory and the Normative Constraint simultaneously.

Now, Davidson does not completely overlook the normative dimension. Instead, he hopes to show that the reasons that explain action may also justify them. He writes:

> In the light of a primary reason, an action is revealed as coherent with certain traits, long- or short-termed, characteristic or not, of the agent, and the agent is shown in his role of Rational Animal. Corresponding to the belief and attitude of a primary reason for an action, we can always construct (with a little ingenuity) the premises of a syllogism from which it follows that the action has some (as Miss Anscombe calls it) "desirability characteristic." Thus there is a certain irreducible—though somewhat anemic sense—in which every rationalization justifies: from the agent's point of view there was, when he acted, something to be said for the action. (Davidson, 1963, pp 690–1)

Whenever you act for a reason, the reason shows, at least from your point of view, at least *one* thing that is to be said in favor of the action. There seems to be at least *this* minimal connection between reasons and normativity.

But the connection between reasons and normativity is not always so anemic. For it is natural to think that—in addition to having reasons that justify what you do—you also have reasons that count in favor of actions that you don't do, nor even want to do. For instance, one might think that people who are boarding a plane that's about to be hijacked have a reason not to board it, even if they are unaware of the impending hijacking, and thus do not have the right belief/pro-attitude pair to count as a "primary reason." Davidson's account of reasons seems to leave us no room to talk about reasons such as this, reasons that would *justify* doing things that an agent, for whatever reason, isn't psychologically equipped to see that she should do.

Can other defenders of psychologism account for this?

Williams and internal reasons

BERNARD WILLIAMS OFFERS a psychologistic framework for thinking about reasons that aims to accommodate some of these concerns. He hopes both to account for how reasons relate to the motives of the agent whose reasons they are, and to account for how reasons are used to critically evaluate what people do and don't do. So it's worth understanding.

But before we examine the details of Williams' view, let's flag a methodological difference between Williams and Davidson. In holding that reasons are belief/pro-attitude pairs, Davidson put forward a thesis about what reasons *are*. He aimed to reduce reasons to psychology. Although Williams also thinks that there is an important connection between reasons and psychology, he is not in the business of telling us what reasons *are*. His goals are more modest. He aims to establish only that when you have a reason to V, it is *necessary* that you have some desire or pro-attitude that V-ing would serve. So, if you have reason to catch the next train out of town, then catching the next train out of town would help you do something you want to do. But this is not a claim directly about what your reason to catch the next train is. Specifically, it is not a claim that your reason to catch the next train *is* some desire of yours. Reasons instead are *based upon* desires.

But *how* are they based upon desires? Williams (1981) claims
that all reasons for action are *internal*; that is, they are grounded
at least in part upon psychological elements internal to the agent
whose reasons they are. Much as Davidson relates all reasons to
pro-attitudes, Williams relates all reasons to *subjective motivations*.
The elements in an agent's subjective motivational set are similarly
diverse; they include wants and desires, stable dispositions to
evaluate things in a particular way, patterns of emotional reaction,
various kinds of commitments and personal loyalties, and so on.
What the elements in this set all have in common in their ability
to motivate the agent whose they are. And an agent's reasons,
Williams thinks, are all related to just such an internal motivation.
There are no *external* reasons, reasons that float completely freely
from how an agent is in fact disposed to be motivated.

Now sometimes, subjective motivations relate to reasons directly,
as when your desire to finish reading this sentence is related to your
reason to finish reading this sentence. Often, however, subjective
motivations relate to reasons indirectly, as when your commitment
to dental health is related to your reason to go to the dentist.
You may neither have nor ever develop *any* motivation to go the
dentist, but the fact that you could be motivated to go the dentist
by soundly deliberating from your current commitment to preserve
your teeth—*this* fact makes it the case that you do indeed have a
reason to go to the dentist. And this is so whether you in fact are
motivated to go to the dentist or not. You have a reason to do not
only what you want to do, but also anything that you could be
motivated to do by soundly deliberating about what to do. And so
you can have a reason to do something that you don't want to do,
to be sure. But you don't have any reasons to act in ways that are
completely unrelated to what you want.

I have been using the notion of *sound deliberation* as though it
were already familiar. But what is it to soundly deliberate from some
subjective motive? Figuring out the means to some end you have
is certainly *one* way to deliberate soundly, as when you determine
to study the rules of the road in order to pass the driving exam. So
is concluding that doing one thing would be a part of some larger
end you have, as when you determine to drive to Atlanta in order
to drive to Miami. And so is specifying how to attain some general
goal of yours, as when you figure out that playing basketball would
be the way to get some exercise—this Williams calls a "constitutive

solution" to one's practical problem. Williams even allows the work of the imagination to count as an instance of sound deliberation. In the end, he is intentionally vague about what does and does not count as sound deliberation, preferring to leave this rather open ended.

One could question whether such vagueness renders Williams' account of reasons trivial. After all, there are some modes of thinking about what to do that could lead *anywhere*: am I soundly deliberating if I open up the dictionary to a random page, close my eyes and point to an entry, and then treat the closest verb listed as though it were a command to be followed? That's certainly a deliberative procedure of some sort, but probably not a sound one. (Not unless it were part of a game that it is rational to play— Milton Bradley, take note.) We want some way of understanding the notion of sound deliberation that does not include procedures like *that*. Even so, Williams' view remains interesting as long as we charitably construe his desire to be open-minded about what counts as sound deliberation. And Williams himself acknowledges that there are some limits here: not just any old bit of deliberation is sound.

We need to note one more feature of Williams' view of reasons for action, one that truly distinguishes his account from Davidson's. You might be unable to be motivated to do something you really have reason to do because you are *unaware* of some consideration that you would need to know in order to do it. If Jacques remains unaware that Mt. Rushmore is near Keystone, South Dakota, he probably isn't going to be motivated to visit Keystone. But if Jacques has a taste for landscape sculpture, then he has a reason to go to Keystone, because he could become motivated to go there were he to become aware of the great monument's location. Likewise, those who don't know how HIV is transmitted still have a reason to use condoms, largely because they could be motivated to use condoms were they to learn how HIV is transmitted and soundly deliberate from there. When we think about what a person's reasons for action are, we may correct for at least some of his false beliefs when we entertain thoughts about what he could be motivated to do. We have reasons to do things about which we are unaware, because we are likewise unaware of many of the ordinary facts relevant to our ends and goals. Our reasons depend upon what we would be motivated to do if we were *well-informed*.

Correcting for ignorance when ascribing reasons must have its limits, though. Most obviously, we may not simply correct for a person's ignorance about *what her reasons are*. Doing that would violate the spirit of the *internal* theory of reasons for action Williams favors. For if an agent becomes aware of her external reasons (should there be any), she then could be motivated to do what she has an external reason to do. To illustrate, suppose you have no motive to take some little blue pill, nor would you be so motivated even if you learned more information about its pharmaceutical and other qualities. You thus have no internal reason to the pill. If you were to have *any* reason at all to take it, it would have to be an external reason. Of course, as things stand, such an external reason cannot motivate you to take it.

But now suppose that somehow (perhaps from the voice of God) you learn that you do indeed have some unspecified reason to take the little blue pill, an external reason if there ever was one. Such a revelation would, it seems, put you into a position to be motivated to take the pill. That is, if God told you that you have a reason to take the pill, then you just might be motivated to take it. And so being informed about external reasons could motivate you to do what you have an external reason to do. Since Williams intends to show that there are no external reasons, he has to rule out this sort of case; while you can have a reason that fails to motivate you because you are unaware of some non-reasons fact (such as how HIV is transmitted), he won't allow ignorance of the reasons themselves to interfere with the motivational power of these reasons.

Some such modification makes sense. When we advise people, we tell them what they have reason to do, and part of what *that* involves is making them aware of things they didn't know. Davidson did not make an analogous move largely because he was concerned specifically with what it is to *act* for a reason, not with what it is to *have* a reason to act. Those who act for reasons are obviously aware (at some level) of their reasons for so acting, but we also have plenty of reasons we never act on. And so it makes sense for their two accounts to differ.

But like Davidson, Williams emphasizes that reasons are always in some way relative to the agent whose reasons they are. Claims about what you have reason to do must be able to get their grip on you. If someone *claims* you have a reason to V, but there is no way for you to be motivated to V by deliberating rationally, then it appears that this claim is *mere bluff*. The person who insists that you really do have a reason to V—even if V-ing would not speak to any pro-attitude you have or could come to have—is essentially trying to bully or trick you into V-ing. And so Williams concludes that in such a situation you don't (or, at least, didn't) really have a reason to V. Reasons are, if not identical to your own psychological attitudes, at least *internal* to them.

Williams defends this claim by asking rhetorically: if claims about your reason to V *aren't* made true by your being already motivated in a way that—with the help of good information and sound deliberation—could lead you to V, then just what, pray tell, *are* claims about your reasons true in virtue of? Williams challenges the opponent of psychologism to produce a superior explanation. Relatedly, Williams asks: when you believe that you have a reason to V, just *what is it* that you thereby believe, if not that you have some motive that could prompt you to V? Again, Williams demands that his opponent offer a better account of the nature of reasons.[4]

Another way to grasp Williams' specific point is to focus on the distinction between the evaluative and the rational. Williams asks us to imagine a very unsavory character who grossly mistreats his wife, a Heartless Husband. (Imagining such a man is, alas, not so difficult.) Williams also asks us to imagine (and this part *is* difficult) that this man has no subjective motive that would be better served by treating his wife well. He really couldn't care less about his wife's well-being. Williams acknowledges and indeed emphasizes that we may say of this man that he is ungrateful, inconsiderate, hard, sexist, brutal, nasty, selfish, and many other things. Many different ways of evaluating him negatively are readily available. And it would clearly be *good* if the man were nicer to his wife. But Williams is reluctant to add that this man also has a *reason* to be nicer to his wife. For whether he does have such a reason depends upon the man's motivations, which, we have already stipulated, do *not* speak in favor of acting more nicely. Reasons are relative to a person's motivations, whereas most evaluations of a person and his activity are not. So Williams invites us to join him in concluding that this very bad man has no reason to be nicer to his wife.

This conclusion might surprise. And it can both impress and disappoint us. Its tendency to *disappoint* stems from standing worries about whether *any* form of belief–desire psychologism can meet the Normative Constraint. We tend to think that people have reasons to do things that need not serve their pre-existing motivations. (We want it to be true that) the Heartless Husband has a reason to treat his wife better. (We want it to be true that) the Heroin Junkie has a reason to stop shooting up. But if reasons are indeed relative to an agent's desires, then there is no guarantee that these things are the case. Williams acknowledges that there is some connection between reasons and normativity, but insists that the connection isn't robust enough to guarantee that immoral or self-destructive people are thereby deficient reasoners. To presume otherwise is, Williams suspects, to think wishfully.

Williams' position can *impress* us in so far as it captures the idea that an agent's reasons are really hers. Even if we doubt he can fully explain the normative dimension of reasons, we might still be moved by Williams' defense enough now to appreciate the sense in which an agent's reasons should not be completely *alien* to her. The reasons that there are for an agent to V must in some sense be *her* reasons. So even if Williams doesn't have all the details right, he is surely correct to think that it is a desideratum of a theory of reasons that it capture the sense in which an agent's reasons are her own. Reasons must be something able to get their grip on *her*, not just something that can elicit a spectator's approval of her. There seems to be more to the thought that something is a reason for you to V than that your V-ing would be somehow good to do.

We also find this idea expressed in the writing of Elizabeth Anscombe, no friend of psychologism. She writes:

> In the philosophy of action we often hear it debated to and fro whether something, *p*, "is a reason" for action. We sometimes hear it said that "moral considerations" *just are* "reasons". But what does all this mean? It seems to be discussed independently of anybody making the thing *his* reason. (Anscombe, 2006, p 146)

We can thus add to our list of desiderata for a theory of reasons. Not only will a successful theory meet the aforementioned Explanatory Constraint and Normative Constraint, accounting for how reasons explain and justify the actions that they are reasons for. It will also meet the *Ownership Constraint*, accounting for how reasons *belong* to the person whose reasons they are. We want to understand how reasons get their grip on the person whose reasons they are, how agents and their reasons are answerable to each other. There *are* such things as unreasonable demands upon people, and it would be a sad state of affairs if our best account of reasons portrayed reasons as making them!

How is the Ownership Constraint any different from the Explanatory Constraint? Both, after all, insist that reasons and agents are related to each other in a particular way. We can see one difference by thinking about an agent who is moved by drives that are not truly his. Suppose Peter is hypnotized to want to eat asparagus ice cream, or to give away his life savings to the Church of Shmientology. If he thus eats some asparagus ice cream, or gives away his life savings to the Church of Shmientology, we will clearly be able to explain his action by mentioning his hypnotically implanted drives. But we should be reluctant to think that Peter has a genuine reason to act so. For there is a sense in which he has such a reason only if it is really *his*. The implanted drive is indeed his in the sense that it is implanted in him, rather than implanted in someone *else*. But it isn't really part of his identity; it is alien to him. In real life, determining whether the operations of some bit of a person's psychology are truly his is often difficult and controversial. Even so, I think we can see the need for some such constraint. Some proposed reason isn't really *your* reason unless it is related to you in 'the right way,' and the mere fact that it can figure in explanations of your actions doesn't suffice to show that it *is* related to you in this way.

So Williams' account of reasons is clearly designed to satisfy both the Explanatory Constraint and the Ownership Constraint, and to improve upon Davidson's attempt to meet the Normative Constraint. But many if not most have found Williams to come up short on this latter goal. To revert to the earlier example, it is natural to think that the Heartless Husband indeed has reasons to treat his wife better, despite his lack of any motivation that doing so would speak to. Sometimes, of course, the response "But I don't care at all about V-ing" adequately defeats any claim that one has a reason to V. But not always. Presumably, the husband in Williams' example promised his wife that he would eternally care for her; they did get married, after all. Even if the husband *no longer* cares about such matters, doesn't the fact that he once promised to treat her well count as a reason for him to do so now? And wouldn't a satisfactory theory of reasons imply that the husband is now unreasonable for being unmoved by such considerations?

Hypotheticalism

PERHAPS THE PSYCHOLOGIST need not fold so quickly. Is there some way for the psychologist to capture the intuition that even the Heartless Husband has a reason to be nicer to his wife? If so, psychologism might not run afoul of the Normative Constraint.

Recently, Mark Schroeder has argued that the psychologist has more resources than is usually recognized (Schroeder, 2008). Schroeder argues, on Humean grounds, that we have surprisingly many reasons for action. His version of psychologism (which he calls Hypotheticalism) is committed to the claim that every time you have a reason for action, you have at least some desire that explains why you have that reason. Schroeder is careful not to say that your desire *is* your reason. The two remain distinct. But Hypotheticalism claims that, for each reason for V-ing you have, you also have *some* desire or other that explains why you have that reason. If there is no relevant desire, then there's just no reason.

How, then, is this compatible with thinking that even the Heartless Husband, who doesn't care at all about his wife, has a reason to be nice to her? Schroeder's strategy is to examine some assumptions about how these desires need to be related to the actions for which one has reasons.

To have a reason to V, you need not desire to V itself. For instance, in order to have a reason to complete your tax return accurately, you need not specifically want to complete your tax return accurately. That would be an odd thing to want for its own sake! If completing your tax return accurately is merely a *necessary means* to something you want, then you have a reason to complete it, even if you don't want to do so. So this shows one way the Humean can agree that you can have reasons to do things that you don't want to do.

Schroeder next points out that some consideration's status as a reason does not really depend upon whether it is a *necessary* means. If there are two equally good ways of doing something you want, then you have a reason to do either. Suppose you want to improve your vision, and the optometrist informs you that you can do so either by wearing contact lenses or by wearing eyeglasses. Even if you don't want to wear eyeglasses, you still have a reason to do so. And even if you don't want to wear contact lenses, you have a reason to do so. (You don't have a reason to wear both, though. That would be not merely redundant, which is bad enough, but counterproductive.) So some means to a desired end need not be strictly necessary in order for you to have some reason to pursue it. Thus just so long as completing your tax return accurately promotes *something* you want, then you have a reason to do it.

But what exactly is it for an action to *promote* an end? Schroeder here argues that we can and should construe this notion very liberally. On his view, an action promotes some outcome just in case performing that action increases the likelihood that the outcome obtains, as compared to the likelihood that the outcome obtains if one does nothing. And this means that you have a reason to V just in case V-ing would make it more likely that something that you want to happen actually happens. We do think that our actions make our ends more likely to occur, and that they do so in ways we foresee and understand. But it's also true that our actions make it more likely that the things that we want obtain in all kinds of ways that we don't foresee.

To illustrate, suppose you would like to have some toothpaste. You thus have a reason to go to the store, because going to the store increases the likelihood that you will have some toothpaste. But going to the store also increases the likelihood that other things that you want to happen will occur. You are more likely to spot a UFO if you go to the store than if you stay at home, and wouldn't you like to spot a UFO? You are more likely to run into your long-lost friend if you go to the store, and wouldn't you enjoy that? There are *all kinds of things* that are more likely to happen if you go to the store. And if you want *any* of them to happen, then you have some reason to go to the store.

Of course, it works the other way too. Staying home, instead of going to the store, increases the likelihood that many things that you want to happen actually happen. If you stay home, you are more likely not to die in an automobile accident. If you stay home, you are more likely to see something interesting on television. And so on. There are all kinds of desired things that are more likely to happen if you stay home.

Now Schroeder's point is that the Humean can persuasively argue that everyone has a reason to observe the rules of morality. For while not everyone wants to act morally, everyone wants *something* whose occurrence is made more likely by acting morally.

For most, this will include prosaic things like avoiding prison and having friends. But there are also countless other desired things that acting morally makes more likely, most of which it is impossible to foretell. Acting morally thus promotes some of your ends. And so long as there is something that you want such that acting morally makes it ever so slightly more likely to take place, then you have a reason to act morally. In fact, your reason to act morally is almost certainly massively overdetermined, given that acting morally will make it more likely that you get *something* that you want.

Schroeder recognizes that this view has some odd implications. Since the promotion relation is so weak, there are many, many reasons to do weird things. Notably, he argues that you even have a reason to eat your car! This is true simply because your car has iron, your body needs iron to be well, and you want to be well. Of course, you would be crazy to (try to) eat your car. You have many, many reasons not to eat your car. And you have only a very tiny reason to do so. So you shouldn't eat it.

Now let's return to the Heartless Husband. Williams accepted that the Heartless Husband did not have a reason to be nicer to his wife, since by hypothesis he does not care at all about her. Many others, including other psychologists, would like to avoid this uncomfortable conclusion. If we understand the promotion relation in the way Schroeder suggests, however, it is overwhelmingly likely that the Heartless Husband has *some* desire that would be promoted by being nicer to his wife. In fact, he probably has very many such desires. And all it takes is one. What's more, it's plausible to think that everyone who is in a position to be nicer to her has some desire such that being nicer to her would promote something desired. In other words, it's plausible that *everyone* has a reason to be nicer to her. The reason to be nicer to her is thus an *agent neutral* reason, since it's a reason that (again, presumably) everyone has.

So, Schroeder concludes that the Humean can capture one of the more important Kantian insight about morality, namely that everyone has a reason to act morally, for acting morally increases the likelihood that at least one desire of each agent is satisfied.

But let's also note one oddity about this account of reasons. If Schroeder's view is right, it may be true that everyone has some reason or other to do what morality requires. The Heartless Husband surely has some desires that can be promoted if he treats his wife better. But one might have thought that the important insight of Kant's is not that everyone has *a* reason to be moral, but that everyone has a *moral* reason to be moral. What's distinctive about morality, Kant proposed, was that it provides its own special type of motivation. Doing the right thing because one is motivated by the wrong sort of inclination is not a case of rational action, in Kant's eyes. Showing that everyone has some incentive to act in ways that happen to comply with morality does not really account for morality's distinctive authority.

This problem does not seem limited to peculiarly moral matters. There are all kinds of actions you can perform only if you have a particular motive. You can't really repent of your crimes unless you actually feel sorry. Saying that you are sorry because it increases the likelihood of something that you want does not constitute repenting. So you can't repent for any old reason. Something similar is true for the act of trusting someone. While there may be a variety of possible motives for trust, you can't trust someone for just any old reason. Rather, to put it roughly, you have to be willing to let some other person have control over some domain that affects your own well-being. Absent this feature, you don't really *trust* the other person, despite whatever else you say or however else you move your body. So while some actions—like treating your wife better—may be performed for strange or ulterior motives, not all actions may be.

Does this pose a problem for Schroeder's view? Perhaps not. Although you may not be able to, say, repent, unless you have some particular motive that you in fact lack, maybe it still can be true that you have reason to repent just in case repenting would in fact get you something that you want. The reason to repent in this case applies to you irrespective of your other motives. It applies to you simply because repenting increases the probability that one of your desires is satisfied, even if this desire isn't motivationally effica-cious. So while you can't genuinely repent for any old reason, you have a reason to repent if doing so would, as matter of fact, make something that you do want more likely to happen.

Let's return, then, to the main thread of the argument. While the Heartless Husband wants to mistreat his wife, and thus has some reasons to do so, he also has a reason to treat his wife nicely. But *which* should he do? It seems that he must weigh these reasons against each other. And the typical method Humeans employ to weigh reasons is to consider the strength of the desires that undergird these reasons: the stronger the desire, the weightier the reason grounded in that desire. This method Schroeder calls Proportionalism, since it holds that the weight of a reason is proportional to the strength of the desire it reflects. In the case of the Heartless Husband, though, Proportionalism has unhappy implications. If his dislike for his wife is strong enough, then this might suggest that his reasons to mistreat her are weightier than his reasons to be nicer to her, which implies that he really should mistreat her. But this does not sound correct—we are back with the unhappy result of Williams' account.

In light of this sort of problem, Schroeder recommends that Humeans reject Proportionalism. While he thinks that desires explain why we have reasons, he does not think that the strength of these desires bears upon how much weight these reasons have. Instead, he proposes a different way to thinking about comparing competing reasons. He thinks that you ought to V just in case it would be *correct* to *place* more weight on the reasons to V than on the reasons not to V. So, Schroeder's view remains plausible if we can make good on the claim that these unpalatable reasons are ones that it is correct not to put much weight upon.

To see whether we can, we need to bring in one very important feature of Schroeder's account that I've ignored so far. Like others, he distinguishes between reasons of the right kind to do something, and reasons of the wrong kind to do something. There can be reasons to do a thing, but they might not be the right kind of reasons to do it. For instance, if I offer to pay you a million dollars to admire me, then it would seem that you then have a reason to admire me, for admiring me would raise the probability that you get many things that you want. But these are not reasons of the right kind to admire me, because there is nothing admirable about offering others money to admire them. (Indeed, it's plausible that you would now have a reason of the right kind *not* to admire me!)

But how do we determine whether a particular reason for action counts as a reason of the right kind? There are different possible answers, but Schroeder's is relatively straightforward and plausible. He claims that "the right kind of reasons involved in any activity are the ones that the people involved in that activity have, *because* they are engaged in that activity" (Schroeder, 2008, p 135). If you are engaged in playing chess, then your reason to move your bishop only diagonally is a reason of the right kind, because this is a reason that you have because you are engaged in playing chess. You might also have a reason to move the bishop horizontally, because it would make your opponent laugh, and that is something that you'd like to make happen. But this is not a reason of the right kind to move your bishop horizontally, because it does not apply to you simply because you are engaged in the activity of chess. Not everyone who is engaged in playing chess shares this reason.

So with this understanding of what a reason of the right kind is, we now can think about what the implications of this distinction are. Schroeder argues that it is correct to place a certain weight on a reason just in case there are reasons of the right kind to place that weight on this reason. This is easiest to grasp by thinking again about our example. The Heartless Husband probably has some reason to abuse his wife: doing so would likely probabilize something that *he* wants. But he also has a reason not to do so, and indeed, to be nicer to her. A moment ago we saw that it is plausible that *everyone* who can help her has some reason or other to be nice to her, for it's likely that being nice to her would probabilize something each person wants.

Now, the Heartless Husband's reason to be nicer to her is weightier than his reason to be abusive to her just in case it is *correct* to place more weight on the former than on the latter. And correctness is determined by reasons of the right kind. So we need to think about what the reasons of the right kind are for the specific activity of placing weight on (other) reasons.

Recall that reasons of the right kind are reasons that everyone engaged in the activity shares just in virtue of being so engaged. And everyone engaged in the specific activity of placing weight on reasons, we think, has a reason to be nice to her. So the reason to be nice to her is a reason of the right kind. But presumably not everyone in the activity of placing weight on reasons has a reason to be abusive to her. So the reason to be abusive to her appears *not* to be a reason of the right kind. Now since there is no reason of the right kind to be abusive to her, while there is indeed a reason of the right kind to be nice to her, it's plausible that it's *correct* to place more weight on the reason to be nice to her than on the reason not to be nice to her. Remember that correctness is determined by only reasons of the right kind, and there presumably is no reason of the right kind *not* to be nice to her.

Thus, although the Heartless Husband may have *some* reason to be abusive to his wife, he doesn't have a reason of the right kind to place weight on this reason. And so it isn't correct for him to place weight on this reason. His reason to be nicer to her, then, is weightier than his reason to be abusive to her, and thus he really should be nicer to her, which is the intuitive result!

Schroeder's alternative to Proportionalism is, however, not so intuitive. Is the real explanation for why the Heartless Husband shouldn't place weight on his reason to be abusive to his wife is that not everyone has such a reason? Would things really be different if everyone *did* have such a reason? It might seem that Hypotheticalism fails to identify *why* it is incorrect to place weight on this reason.

Here's a related but different problem with Hypotheticalism. As we've seen, given that the Heartless Husband wants all kinds of different things, he surely has some reason or other to be nicer to his wife. In fact, he probably has lots and lots of reasons to be nicer to her, most of which are not obvious. But this is not the only relevant action for which there's an operative reason. If Schroeder is correct about the way reasons work, then it's clear that the Heartless Husband also has a reason to *kill* his wife. In fact, he probably has lots and lots of reasons to kill her. Killing her would make many different things that he wants more likely to happen, even though most of these ways are also not obvious.

Schroeder's strategy in response should be to point out that the weight of the Husband's reason to kill her may be very small, and so it plays no significant role in determining what the Husband has most reason to do. But there is a real question whether Hypotheticalism actually yields this result.

Consider that it's not only agents like the Heartless Husband who can increase the likelihood of something wanted by killing a family member. It's true for you and me as well. As uncomfortable as it might be to acknowledge, killing your family would make many (though far from most) things that you want somewhat more likely to happen, mostly in ways that aren't easily foreseeable. For instance, killing your family may increase the likelihood that you understand how much you love(d) them, and don't you want to understand that? It might also further population control, and this too might be something that you want. More generally, it seems just as likely that killing your family would probabilize something you want, as that being nice to his wife would probabilize something that the Heartless Husband wants.

Thus, the weakness of the promoting relation cuts both ways. By making reasons nearly ubiquitous, Schroeder's Hypotheticalism can accommodate the idea that even the most wicked of villains has a reason to be moral, but it equally supports the conclusion that everyone also has a reason to act in all kinds of evil and twisted ways. In attempting to show how we all have reasons to act morally, we have shown that we all have reasons to act immorally too. Further, since it seems to be true that *everyone* has both a reason to be moral and a reason to be evil, both of these reasons count as reasons of the right kind. So this seems like it might be a huge problem.

Much the same can be said for cases involving prudence (self-interest). The weakness of the promoting relation supports the conclusion that everyone has some reason or other to do what's in her own interest, for promoting this would surely make it more likely that at least one of her own desires is thereby satisfied. Yet at the same time, the weakness of the promoting relation also supports the conclusion that everyone has some reason or other to end her own life, for promoting this would likewise make it more likely that at least one of her own desires is thereby satisfied. And since it seems to be true that everyone has both a reason to be prudent and to commit suicide, both of these reasons count as reasons of the right kind. And this too is a highly counterintuitive conclusion.

So it remains difficult to see how desire-based psychologism can meet the Normative Constraint. Being reasonable might not be identical to being wise, but plausibly the reasonable person is sensitive to both ethical and prudential considerations, and tends to respond positively to them. Perhaps defenders of desire-based psychologism can still find some way to meet the Normative Constraint, or can convincingly argue that the Normative Constraint really isn't a desideratum. Nothing I've argued here has shown that they cannot. But until then, we should note that desire-based psychologism seems to meet some but not all of the various things we want from a theory of reasons.

Our real question, though, is not whether desire-based psychologism is free of flaws. It's whether desire-based psychologism is superior to its alternatives.

CHAPTER THREE

Psychologism: beliefs

Reasons for action are probably not based upon belief–desire pairs. A more promising strategy might be to investigate whether reasons for action are based upon beliefs alone. Believing that a course of action would be fun, prudent, or kind might itself be a reason so to act.

To explore the plausibility of this idea, we will see whether the belief model is superior to the belief–desire model. First, we will continue to undermine the belief–desire model by seeing that beliefs-and-desires are not always sufficient for reasons. Of course, showing this does not demonstrate that beliefs alone can be reasons. But it does call into question the importance of desires. We will then look at several contemporary proposals supporting the idea that beliefs alone are sometimes sufficient for grounding reasons for action. Finally, we will consider a couple arguments against all forms of psychologism.

The anti-sufficiency point

THE NORMATIVE CONSTRAINT instructs us to capture the idea that reasons have normative force. Psychologistic accounts of reasons that identify or base reasons upon pro-attitudes (Davidson),

subjective motives (Williams), or desires (Schroeder) appear to fail
to meet this Constraint in two ways. First, as in the case of the
Heartless Husband, it seems that a person can have a reason to do
something that fails to serve any of his pro-attitudes or subjective
motives. It seems that pro-attitudes aren't necessary for reasons.
Let's call this the anti-necessity point.

Second, it also seems you can have a pro-attitude toward doing
something for which you have no reason for doing. That is, it seems
that pro-attitudes aren't sufficient for reasons. Let's call this the
anti-sufficiency point. We will examine the anti-sufficiency point in
this section.

Is it true that having a desire (and a belief) with suitable contents
suffices to generate a reason to do the thing desired?

A provocative example of Davidson's illustrates the very
problem. Davidson asks us to imagine a man who has a lifelong
yen to drink a can of paint (1963, p 686). The man need never
actually think that indulging this bizarre urge would be in any way
good to do; he's not *that* crazy. But suppose that the man yields
to its prompting, opens the lid, and begins drinking the paint. The
Davidsonian seems committed to saying that the man was drinking
the can of paint for a reason: he had a yen to do so. But while the
correct explanation of the man's behavior will surely cite his odd
craving, admitting this is not equivalent to acknowledging that the
man's urge is identical to or is the ground of any reason to which
he was responding by drinking the can of paint. We may think that
the man had no reason to drink the paint at all—and if we do think
this, then this is likely because we think that, *as the man himself
does*, that drinking paint isn't the thing to do. Not every behavior
prompted by an urge is an action undertaken for a reason. People
can behave weirdly. Call this objection to desire-based theories of
reasons *the paint-drinking objection*.[1]

We find two different sorts of replies to the paint-drinking
objection. The first presses the point that the paint-drinker indeed
has *some* justification for giving in to his urge. Desires really are
sufficient for reasons. But we can avoid biting bullets by divorcing
the normative strength of reasons from the motivational strength of
desires. That is, even if the man has a very strong urge (and thus *a*
reason) to drink a can of paint, the strength of the reason need not
be as strong as the urge. The strength of the reason may be *very*
small indeed. So his powerful yen to drink a can of paint grounds

only a very weak reason to drink a can of paint. And this weak reason is surely wildly outweighed by his many reasons *not* to drink the paint. So if in the end he *is* unduly motivated by this very weak reason to drink the can of paint, there is still a sense in which he's acting unreasonably, for he is insufficiently sensitive to the bulk of his reasons with respect to paint-drinking. This proposal thus shows how a desire-based theory of reasons can preserve a link between reasons and normativity, without thereby committing itself to any wildly unintuitive implications about when people act unreasonably.

But one might bristle at the implication that the paint-drinker has *any* reason whatsoever to drink a can of paint, even an infinitesimally weak one. It is not easy to discern a fair way to judge which view—no reason or an infinitesimally weak one—is correct. Our intuitions are not always so sharp or fine grained.[2]

The second sort of reply to the paint-drinking objection is much more interesting. It grants that the paint-drinker may have no justification whatsoever for drinking the paint. After all, even from this paint-drinker's point of view, there's nothing *good* about drinking paint. But would acknowledging this really commit us to the view that the paint-drinker has no *reason* to drink the paint?

One might argue, *pace* the Normative Constraint, that reasons for action need not have any normative force. We might think that it's one thing to be a reason, and it's something else altogether to be a *good* reason. *Good* reasons, of course, have normative force. But reasons unqualified often do not. And so, on this view, you can act for a reason that has no normative element or quality. Doing what you have reason to do might be unambiguously bad.

This reply does not even grant Davidson's concession that every reasons-explanation justifies, if only in the anemic sense that—from the agent's point of view—there is something to be said for the action. Perhaps you can act for a reason without thinking that there's *anything* good or justifiable about you so acting. On this view, the following dialogue is perfectly coherent:

A: What the hell are you doing?
B: I'm drinking a can of paint. You got a problem with that?
A: Drinking a can of *paint*? You know that's paint, and you're drinking it anyway! *[exasperated]* Why on earth are you doing that?
B: I just have an urge to drink it. That's all.

A: How weird. I don't see why anyone would *want* to drink paint. What's so good about drinking paint?

B: Good?! There's nothing *good* about drinking a can of paint.

A: Then for what reason are you doing it?

B: I told you: because I have an urge to drink it.

A: Yeah, but do you have an urge to chop off your toes? Why not? Because there'd be no point to chopping off your toes—*that's* why not. There'd be nothing good about it. But then why drink paint if there's nothing good about it?

B: *[glug] [gag]*

A: Is this some weird Freudian thing?

B: No!

A: Is this some sort of political protest against the petroleum industry?

B. Nah.

A: Maybe some performance art piece about making the insides of the artist's body the "canvas"?

B: Hey, that's a good one, but I can't say I thought of that.

A: Does it get you high ... like sniffing glue?

B: Not in my experience.

A: Do you want to kill yourself?

B: No! Look. I know it's completely stupid, but I just have an urge to drink paint, OK? And your yammering on doesn't make me feel any better. If you want to do me some good, you would shut up and wrestle this paint can away from me so that I don't drink any more of it ... I'm only a couple fluid ounces in to it so far. Maybe if I had a straw ...

Clearly, B doesn't want to drink paint for any *further* reason. And it appears that B doesn't see anything good about drinking paint. The question, then, is whether it's possible for B to drink paint for the mere reason that he wants to drink paint, a reason that is in no way connected to what's good or justifiable, even by his own lights. Can his urge alone—construed as cut off from any belief about what's good—constitute a practical reason? This question might be answered negatively on several different grounds. Here are five possibilities, each briefly sketched.

1 Not an *action*. B might drink the paint because of his urge to drink some paint, but if so, B's drinking some paint—though a bit of behavior—isn't an full-blooded intentional action, and so falls outside the scope of our inquiry. So urges can indeed cause mere behavior, but such behavior doesn't rise to the level of action. Behavior caused by urges isn't the sort of thing that there are reasons for or against.

2 Not a *reasons* explanation. B might drink the paint because of his urge to drink paint, and B's drinking the paint is an action, but if so, this explanation for why he is drinking the paint isn't thereby a reasons explanation of his action. Even psychologists should acknowledge that not every explanation whose explanans is a psychological attitude counts as a reasons explanation. Rather, B's urge to drink paint explains why B drinks paint in much the same way that one's horrible headache can explain why one is pulling at one's ears. Sometimes our states of mind make us *do* things, and those states of mind explain *why* we do what we do, but those states are not reasons *for which* we do them. So the fact that B's drinking paint was caused by B's urge fails to show that urges ground reasons for action.

3 Not a *reason*. B might be motivated to drink paint simply by his urge to do so, without seeing anything good about drinking paint, but then his urge isn't a reason for action. He acts for no reason, which isn't to say that his action is not intentional. One can act intentionally for no reason, as one does when one doodles idly, or drums one's fingers on the table.

4 Not a *known* reason. B may be motivated to drink paint simply by his urge to do so, but despite his protests that he sees nothing good about drinking paint, at some level he must see something good about drinking paint: for instance, he finds the creamy appearance of paint pleasant, or drinking paint affirms his iconoclasm. If he were more self-aware and articulate, then he could characterize the desirability of drinking paint in some comprehensible way. For to want something is to respond to some perceived or imagined desirable characteristic of the thing wanted. On this view, desires themselves are directed at what's good, so of course actions motivated by reasons constituted by such desires are also connected to what's good. So we need not think that B's unresponsiveness to A's questions indicates anything other than a failure of self-awareness and/or articulacy. Although B does act for a reason, he doesn't act for a reason that's divorced from all considerations of what's good. We can act for reasons that to some extent aim to justify what we do, even if we feel that we are at a loss to see or to say just how this is so.

5 Not a *typical* reason. B might be motivated to drink paint simply by his urge to do so, and this urge might even be his reason for drinking paint, and this urge might be in no way directed to or connected with any perceived or imagined good about the object of the urge, but this is somehow a degenerate case. It couldn't be the case that the reasons for which agents act are *typically* not good, or at least good in the eyes of the agent herself. There *can* be unusual instances of someone acting for a reason that even the agent fails to see as good in any way. Thus this fifth response is somewhat concessive. But this unusual instance is possible only in the order of a larger context in which there's a connection between reasons for action and goodness (Boyle and Lavin, 2010).

(Here's a shaky analogy. It's no accident that creatures with functioning hearts are also creatures with functioning kidneys. Generally, if a creature has a heart, it has kidneys too. But it's possible for there to be a creature that has a functioning heart but lacks functioning kidneys. Sometimes Nature misfires, or the environment wreaks havoc, or biological entropy overwhelms us. Even so, the strong positive correlation between creatures with hearts and creatures with kidneys is not merely coincidental or statistical. The existence of heart-creatures without kidneys asymmetrically depends [in a way] upon the fact that there are creatures with both hearts and kidneys. So too, the existence of reasons for action unconnected with goodness asymmetrically depends [in a way] upon the existence of reasons that *are* connected with goodness.)

Which of these five responses, if any, is the right thing to say? I believe that each response is initially somewhat plausible. And the five responses aren't mutually exclusive; more than one could be true. All cast doubt on the claim that acting on an urge that is in no way connected to what's good is, without qualification, acting for a reason. This conclusion can be strengthened by glancing over at analogous issues concerning reasons for believing.

Suppose B believes that the next world war will begin on a Wednesday. When A asks B why, B only can respond that he has a *hunch*, where a hunch is supposed to be the theoretical equivalent of an urge. B acknowledges that he doesn't have any *further* reasons for believing that the next world war will begin on a Wednesday. And he also acknowledges that there's nothing "intuitive" or intrinsically credible to the idea that the next world war will begin on a Wednesday. He can tell that it sounds crazy to believe such a thing. But he does believe it—he insists he really does. Is his hunch a reason for him to believe this?

We can consider analogous versions of the same five responses:

1 Not a *belief*. B doesn't really believe that the next world war will begin on a Wednesday. If he has only a hunch about this, then while he may suspect or feel drawn to the thought that the next world war will begin on a Wednesday, he doesn't genuinely believe it. To say that he doesn't believe it is not to say anything about the strength of B's feelings. It's instead to say something about the kind of psychological attitude B has. Beliefs are held for reasons, such as evidence. If B doesn't believe that the next world war will begin on a Wednesday for a reason, then B just doesn't believe that. And so, B's hunch is not a reason for belief.

2 Not a *reasons explanation*. B might believe that the next world war will begin on a Wednesday because (in some sense) of his hunch, but this is not a case of believing something *for a reason*. Instead, B's hunch explains B's belief in some other way. Perhaps B's hunch merely *causes* or otherwise somehow explains B's belief that the next world war will begin on a Wednesday. But when mere hunch-like feelings lead to beliefs, they don't explain beliefs in the way that reasons do in reasons explanation.

3 Not a *reason*. B might believe that the next world war will begin on a Wednesday, and he does so simply because of a hunch, but his hunch is not a reason. Not every belief is held for a reason. Which isn't to say that B doesn't genuinely believe this. You can believe something for no reason.

4 Not a *known* reason. B might believe that the next world war will begin on a Wednesday, and he believes this simply because of a hunch, and this hunch is indeed his reason for believing this. But despite his protestations, he must at some level see (or think he sees) something intuitive about this hunch: for instance, he finds the alliteration contained in the thought that a world war will begin on a Wednesday a sign that such an event is fated. Or, at some level he thinks that people tend to get bored or cranky in the middle of the work-week, and that this makes Wednesday belligerency probable. To believe something is to respond to perceived or imagined evidence favoring the thing believed. We need not think that B's unresponsiveness to A's questions indicates anything other than a failure of articulacy and/or self-awareness.

5 **Not a *typical* reason**. B might believe that the next world war will begin on a Wednesday, and he believes this simply because of a hunch, and this hunch is indeed his reason for believing this, but this is somehow a degenerate case. It couldn't be the case that the reasons for which people believe things are *typically* mere hunches. There can be *unusual* instances of someone believing something for a reason that she fails to see as evidence in any way for the truth of what she believes. But this is possible only in the order of a larger context in which there's a general connection between reasons for belief and truth.

Each of these five possible responses initially seems somewhat plausible. And they are not mutually exclusive; more than one might be true.

The analogy between unreasoned urges and unreasoned hunches extends further. It *can* be reasonable, in a sense we haven't yet explored, to do something just because you have an urge to do it, and to believe something just because you have a hunch about it. For suppose you know that your previous urges and hunches about how things stand in some domain have been surprisingly reliable.

Some people, for instance, apparently have reliable opinions about the sex of the chicks they examine. This can be a useful skill, as the economic value of a female chick is far greater than that of a male, and so farmers often want to kill the males and raise only the females. But at least some of these chicken-sexers are unable to say why they believe that any particular chick they examine is female or male. It's not fully understood how all chicken-sexers form their opinions; the sex organs of a young chick are completely internal, and so aren't visibly obvious. And so some chicken-sexers don't know *why* they believe what they do, don't know anything beyond that they believe a particular examined chick is, say, a female because the chick *is* a female.

In other words, these professional chicken-sexers have hunches. These opinions count as *hunches* because often they have no specific idea *how* they determine what the sex of a particular chick is. Now in this case, it might be thought that a professional chicken-sexer's hunch is a reason for belief, for she knows that her hunches about such matters have usually been accurate. Trusting her hunches makes sense. It seems like the reasonable thing for her to do. But the only candidate reason seems to be her hunch. So perhaps her hunch just is her reason: when asked why she believes that some particular chick is, say, male, she is likely to answer only that she has a hunch that it is.

How should we think about the parallel case for urges? Suppose someone knows that in the past when she has acted from urges, she usually winds up acting well. It is sometimes said that some pregnant women have seemingly blind urges to eat foods containing needed nutrients, but that they aren't aware that they have any nutritional deficiencies that their urges aim to remedy. They simply feel the urges. A woman pregnant with her fourth child might then eat some specific food she is craving, because she thinks that indulging her earlier pregnancy cravings contributed to the birth of three healthy children, and so she now trusts her dietary urges while pregnant with her fourth child. If she now has the urge to eat, say, raw jalapeño peppers, she does so. Just as it's reasonable for a professional chicken-sexer to trust her hunches about the sex of the chicks she examines, so too it's reasonable for the veteran mother to trust her urges about what to eat. This might lead us to feel comfortable concluding that her urge to eat raw jalapeño peppers is a reason for her to eat raw jalapeño peppers.

But there is reason to resist this conclusion. Although the chicken-sexer is unable to *say* any more about why she categorizes chicks as she does than that she has a hunch, it's clear that her ability to know the sex of chicks has something to do with her *perceptual* abilities. She does not intellectually intuit the correct answer in the way that a psychic allegedly does. God does not whisper the answer into her ear. She is not implementing some wildly successful chick-counting system in the way that a professional blackjack player predicts the next card based upon the cards already played. She perceives—most likely sees or feels rather than hears or smells—*something* about the chick that grounds her opinion that the chick is, say, a male. She can't articulate this ground, either due to an impoverished vocabulary, a lack of self-awareness, or—what's most likely—some deficit that stems from the combination of the two. But it seems natural to say that she has some further reason for thinking that this chick is a male. The problem is we just don't know what the further reason is. The hunch isn't itself the reason, it's the subjective shadow of the reason we would like to pin down.

Urges that seem sensible to indulge can, like some hunches, be responses to obscure features of their objects. These obscure features to which the agent is responding may be, in the case of urges, good in respects that register with her. Although she may be unable to *say* any more about why she wants to eat raw jalapeno peppers than that she has an urge to do so, it's clear that her propensity to be drawn toward eating peppers has something to do with the way her appetite is affected by her body's needs. She does not intellectually adopt the urge. God does not implant this urge in her. But she seems to be responding to some genuinely good aspect of the object of her craving. She can't articulate the nature of its goodness, but it seems natural to say that she has some further reason for eating raw jalapeno peppers. The problem is we just don't know what the further reason is. The urge isn't itself the reason, it's the subjective shadow of the reason we would like to pin down.

We could say much more about whether all reasons for action must be at least aimed at what's good, and so cannot be based simply on desires that have no such aim. As we will see in Chapter 5, those who sharply distinguish motivating reasons from normative reasons sometimes argue that only normative reasons aim at the good, freeing up motivating reasons to be based upon desires that need not aim at the good. We will tackle that view then.

For now, note that having a desire alone, unconnected to any view about the object of desire being good in any way, seems not to ground a practical reason. And so it appears that you can desire to do something without thereby having any reason to do it.

The anti-necessity point

Desiring to do something seems not *sufficient* for having a reason to do it. Now let's consider whether having a relevant desire is *necessary* for having a practical reason, or if beliefs alone can do the trick.

Is it really true that you have a reason to V only if you already have some desire, pro-attitude, or subjective motive that V-ing will serve? If so, then morality, prudence, and every other normative system rationally bind you only if you happen to have the relevant desires. And so because it can seem that the rational authority of at least some normative systems does *not* turn on what you want, we might conclude that you have a reason to do that which you know is wise or courageous, even if you don't want to do what's wise or courageous. Having a reason doesn't always depend upon what you want. Or so it can seem. We'll look at a couple arguments in support of this thought shortly.

But first, let's briefly articulate one grave doubt about whether we can jettison desires here. We do things for reasons. But it may seem we can act for a reason only if we in some sense desire to so act. Denying that desires are necessary for reasons seems to amount to embracing the possibility that we can act for a reason simply when we have only the appropriate *belief*. For instance, can you schedule an appointment with your dentist simply because you think that it would be healthy for you to do so, irrespective of whether you want to be healthy? Can beliefs alone play the motivational role played by reasons?

Defenders of the belief–desire model, owing much to Hume, often argue that beliefs cannot play this motivational role. The Explanatory Constraint says that reasons for action must be able to explain the actions for which they are reasons. If I am asked why I'm writing a book, I will explain why by citing my reasons. But beliefs alone cannot explain why I am doing what I am. Beliefs alone are motivationally inert. They aim to represent the way the world is, but they do not aim to change the way the world is. So a belief all by itself is just the wrong sort of thing to explain action. And since reasons for action must be able to explain action, a belief alone cannot be a reason for action.

But is it really true that beliefs about reasons are inadequate to explain the actions for which they are reasons? It is likely that garden-variety beliefs are not enough: my belief that there is beer in the refrigerator is not all by itself a reason for me to do anything. But beliefs with special content—content about morally or prudentially relevant subject matter—might work differently.

Let's consider several different specific accounts of reasons that maintain that reasons need not be grounded in desires. Some remain psychologistic; some do not. We can order these accounts according to the degree to which they deviate from the basic Humean picture.

The first variant to consider was initially clearly formulated by Thomas Nagel (1971). Nagel maintains that not all of your reasons for actions are grounded upon your current desires. You have reasons to do things—and thus can be motivated to do things—that you don't have a pre-existing desire to do. A fortiori, not all reasons are based on desires. Nagel instead thinks that some reasons for action are based upon beliefs alone. This is clearest and most important in cases when you have reason to do something now that will benefit either yourself in the future, or another person, even when you don't now care about such things.

To argue for these claims, Nagel distinguishes between *motivated desires* and *unmotivated desires*. Unmotivated desires are desires that an agent just finds herself with. If you are suddenly struck with a craving for chicken vindaloo, your desire is not the result of any rational deliberation: you are at least initially passive in the face of it. Many bodily desires are similarly unmotivated; our animality is a rich source of drives, urges, and wants. But many desires that are not obviously somatic can also be unmotivated: for instance, a person can just be in the mood to play chess.

Many if not most desires, however, are motivated by deliberation. Suppose you want something to drink, and you have a dollar in your pocket. You might be motivated to put your dollar in a nearby soda machine. If so, you have a desire to put your dollar in the nearby soda machine, a desire that is motivated by the thought that doing so will get you something to drink. Your desire to insert the dollar into the machine does not strike you from out of the blue. *That* would be a very odd urge! Instead, your desire to put the dollar into the machine can be rationally explained, by the same thing that also explains the action of putting the dollar in the machine. This kind of explanation is, then, a motivating explanation, and so the desire to put the dollar in the machine is a motivated desire.

Note that typically you can't tell whether a particular desire is a motivated desire or an unmotivated desire just by considering its content. A desire to eat an orange might either suddenly strike you, or you may be motivated by the thought that eating an orange is a way of getting Vitamin C.

The distinction between motivated desires and unmotivated desires echoes Plato's distinction between rational desire and appetitive desires. Nagel similarly distinguishes between motivated desires and unmotivated desires in order to argue that not all reasons are, or are based upon, desires. He notes that whenever you act for a reason, it is true that you *have* a desire. But sometimes the reason explains both your action and your desire. For instance, in the above example, when you put a dollar in the machine for a reason, it is perfectly correct to ascribe to you a desire to put a dollar in the machine. That desire-ascription is correct simply in virtue of the fact that you put a dollar in the machine for a reason. But that ascribed desire does no real explanatory work. What explains your action is the same thing that explains your desire: your knowing that putting a dollar in the machine is a way of getting something to drink. So Nagel agrees with Davidson that whenever you act for a reason, you *have* some relevant desire or pro-attitude. There is no rational motivation without a desire *present*. But according to Nagel, you have this desire for the same reason that you act for—the desire is not (part of) the reason; the reason here instead explains the desire.

The Davidsonian will be quick to point out that in Nagel's example, the reason for which you drop a dollar in the soda machine, *does* rest upon a desire: the desire to drink something. So while it may be true that the desire to put a dollar in the machine is "merely ascribed," the desire to drink something is a crucial element of the reason for putting the dollar in the machine. The desire to drink something is not merely ascribed. So even if some desires are not the reasons for which we act, it still might be true that every reason for action originates in and indeed contains a desire.

In order to show that at least some reasons do *not* rest upon such a desire, Nagel focuses attention on reasons of prudence.[3] Let's consider another unusual example of his. Imagine that in six weeks you will be in Rome. Then, as you now know, you will have reason to be able to speak Italian. You, alas, do not now know

Italian. So it is very plausible that you now have a reason to learn some Italian. But suppose you don't want to learn Italian, nor—bizarrely—want anything that knowing Italian in six weeks will accomplish. Learning Italian now serves no present desire of yours. Yet, you know full well that in six weeks you will have reason to be able to speak some Italian. It isn't as though you now believe that in six weeks you will mistakenly think you have a reason to speak Italian. Rather, you now grant that you *will* indeed have such a reason. But does the fact that you now lack the right kind of desire defeat the claim that you now have a reason to learn Italian?

Nagel argues that to be unmotivated to learn Italian now is to be dissociated from yourself six weeks hence. It's as though the person who will be in Rome in six weeks is not the same person as you. Failing to regard your foreseen future reason to speak Italian as providing you with a reason now to learn Italian is failing to identify with yourself. There is thus an important connection between your identity and your reasons. It is correct to regard yourself not as an agent who exists only in the present moment (if that's even a coherent thing to imagine), but as someone who has existed, does exist, and will exist. Because you exist not just at a particular point in time, neither do your reasons for acting. Your reasons are, Nagel argues, *timeless*. If at any point in time you have a reason to do something, then you have that reason timelessly. If the consideration in question is in the past, you now may have only reason to regret (or appreciate) what you did. But if the consideration lies in the future, you now have reason to take steps to promote the relevant goal or end. Thus if in six weeks you will have a reason to speak Italian, that reason is also relevant to you now, even if you don't feel much like doing anything about it. The existence of reasons does not depend, then, on the existence of a present desire.

There are several different plausible critical responses to Nagel's argument, even if we accept his analysis of this example. First off, even supposing that reasons don't depend upon the existence of a present desire, they still seem to depend upon the existence of a future desire—in this case, your desire in six weeks to speak Italian. This result might still warm the Davidsonian's heart.

In response, Nagel might emphasize that in this example, since the relevant desire is in the future, there need be no desire *rationally motivating* you now to learn Italian. Rather, the belief that you will be in Italy six weeks hence is *alone* supposedly sufficient to motivate you to learn Italian immediately. If your future desire is somehow relevant to the existence of your present reason, this may be only because satisfaction of your future desire is in your interest or well-being, and you have a reason to do what's in your interest. So Nagel can admit that your future desire is not entirely irrelevant to whether you have a reason now to learn Italian. But this might simply be because you have a reason to do what's good for you, and one of the things that is good for you is to have your future desires fulfilled. This wouldn't directly connect reasons and desires; reasons need not be directly dependent upon desires in order for this to be true. So Nagel could argue that the marriage of a non-Humean theory of reasons with a desire-satisfaction theory of well-being can make sense of the example.

It's important to see that while Nagel attempts to demonstrate that desires need not explain rational action, he often writes as though beliefs still do. Since he thinks that beliefs rationally motivate action, there is a sense in which he thinks that beliefs *are* reasons. That is, on Nagel's view, it makes perfect sense to say that the reason you are learning Italian now is that you *believe* that in six weeks you will be in Italy. And this makes it appropriate to view Nagel's view as a version of psychologism.

But are beliefs really reasons? Many anti-Humeans think that Nagel does not move far enough away from psychologism. Nagel rejects the Humean thought that reasons must depend upon desires, but, like Hume, still seems to hold that they depend upon psychological attitudes. But once one rejects this bit of psychologism on the ground that desires aren't necessary for reasons, it becomes natural to question whether beliefs too are really necessary.

In the next chapter, we will investigate some positive accounts that reasons are not psychological. Right now, we will look into a more ambitious way of tying reasons to cognitive attitudes.

Reasons as ideal beliefs

THE ANTI-NECESSITY point is the claim that not every reason is, or is grounded by, a desire. But to accept the anti-necessity point is not necessarily to deny reasons are related to *some* psychological attitude or other. The theoretical task then becomes to account for why some but not other attitudes are sources of reasons. One common move is to deny only that the attitude in question must belong to the very agent whose reason it is. Perhaps reasons are related to the attitudes of agents we should aspire to.

There are several different ways one might go about this. John McDowell has argued that a person has reason to do whatever a *wise and virtuous* person in those circumstances would think to do (McDowell, 1979). (This puts the matter a little too simply, but it conveys the most important point.) Your reasons are sensitive not to your own psychological attitudes but to those of a wise person. McDowell describes the relevant psychological element of a wise person as her *conception of how to live*. A conception of how to live, though cognitive, is much more grandiose than a garden-variety belief. This conception is an uncodifiable view about how one is to live one's life—uncodifiable, because it cannot be captured in any finite set of expressible rules or principles. Further, the wise person's conception of how to live is both belief-like and desire-like. It is like a belief in that it embodies a view about how one is to live, a view that can be correct or incorrect. And it is like a desire in that it directly motivates the wise person to live according to its vision. The Davidsonian appears to presume that psychological attitudes can be either beliefs or desires but never both. McDowell basically rejects this thought; he holds that one and the same psychological attitude can be both cognitive and conative.

Resistance to McDowell's stance can be fueled by the worry that we need to be able to distinguish sharply between the cognitive and the conative in order to understand the difference between two people with the same ideal but different motivations. Two people might share the same conception of how to live, but only one of the two bothers to live in accordance with their shared conception. What can explain the difference in behavior except for the possibility that only one person *wants* to live as they both think they should? It can seem necessary to ascribe some (additional) desire to the person who does as he thinks he should.

McDowell's solution for defusing this worry is clever. He acknowledges that there must be some psychological difference between the person who lives as she thinks she should and the person who does not. In fact, he also acknowledges that there must be some psychological difference between the person who acts as she thinks she should in the face of temptation, and the person who does the same without any internal conflict—in Aristotle's awkward terms, between the temperate and the merely continent.[4] But McDowell aims to explain these differences not by ascribing an extra desire to the person who acts as she thinks she should, but by ascribing an extra desire to the person who does *not* act as she thinks she should. He says that a person who is not directly motivated to act according to her conception of how to live is probably blinded by a desire that interferes with her ability to see matters clearly. Desires thus not only can motivate us to act, they also derail or obscure otherwise powerful motivations. On this view, the difference between our two agents does have something to do with a presence of a desire, but it's the comparably foolish person who has the extra desire, not the fully practically rational and wise person.

McDowell could mean two different things here. On the one hand, he might mean that the presence of an extra desire interferes with the less-than-fully-wise agent's ability to grasp the wise person's conception of how to live, an ability that the agent *would* exercise successfully were it not for the desire's distraction. Our ordinary agent's conception of how to live, on this reading, at best only approximates the conception of how to live had by the wise person. On the other hand, McDowell might mean that the presence of an extra desire interferes with only the motivational power of the conception of how to live grasped equally well by both the wise person and the less-than-fully wise person. According to this reading, two agents can share the same view of how to live, but its motivational power can be blocked by other non-rational psychological factors. I suspect that McDowell intends only the first interpretation, a view that should seem familiar—Plato himself portrayed the irrational person as someone whose unruly appetites prevent one for seeing what the wise person sees. But some of McDowell's remarks at least suggest the second interpretation too. (Note that the positions described by the two interpretations aren't mutually exclusive.)

The substance of the second interpretation of McDowell's view is presented more straightforwardly by Christine Korsgaard, who argues that reasons normally or typically have motivational force, but that this force can be blocked by any of a wide variety of interfering factors: "[r]age, passion, depression, distraction, grief, physical or mental illness: all these things could cause us to act irrationally, that is, to fail to be motivationally responsive to the rational considerations available to us" (1986, p 13). That is, reasons motivate us only in so far as we ourselves are rational. The presence of irrational factors such as those listed above can defeat the efficacy of reasons. Reasons, then, can be inherently motivating, even if they are not perfectly or omnipotently so. Non-rational desires and emotions can get in the way. No doubt they often do.

Korsgaard argues this not to defend a picture of reason wherein reason can motivate a person to act no matter how he is otherwise disposed. Such a picture of reason's powers would strike us as far-fetched. Instead, she offers a model of practical reason wherein reason ensures that one has specific motives. On this model, you need not have any *rationally optional* desires in order to have practical reasons.

To illustrate, let's look at a very simple example from the sphere of reasons for belief. Suppose that you believe p. Suppose also that you believe q. You might then come to believe p&q. If you do, then this is likely because you also "believe in" conjunction. But such a belief is not quite like the belief that p, or the belief that q—beliefs that are probably rationally optional. Believing in conjunction, by contrast, isn't rationally optional. Every rational thinker believes in conjunction, at least implicitly so. Those who don't are, to that extent, poor reasoners. So although we may represent the belief in conjunction as one of many beliefs in your set of beliefs, its status clearly matters in way that most of your beliefs do not.

We find something similar at work in the domain of practical reason. Suppose that you are strongly attached to some benign particular end E. Suppose that you believe that M-ing is necessary to attain end E, and there are no drawbacks to M-ing. You might then M. If you do M, then this is likely because you also are motivated to take the necessary means to your ends, because you in some sense 'endorse' the means–end principle. But such an endorsement is not quite like your attachment to end E—an attachment that could be rationally optional. Accepting the means-end principle, by contrast, *isn't* rationally optional. Every rational agent endorses the means–end principle, at least implicitly so. Those who don't are, to that extent, poor reasoners. So although we may represent your endorsement of the means–end principle as one of many elements in your subjective motivational set, its status clearly matters in way that most of your motives do not.

What goes for the means–end principle might go for more ambitious ideas about the content of practical reason. If all rational agents are motivated to take the means toward the end, perhaps it also can be successfully argued that all rational agents are motivated to act for the sake of their future well-being, or for the sake of the well-being of others. Korsgaard is careful not to assume that she can just help herself to these conclusions. It would take some daunting metaphysical arguments to establish them (see Korsgaard, 1996; Korsgaard, 2008). Right here, her point instead is that once it is granted that all rational people have *some* specific traits that can motivate (e.g. endorsement of the means/end principle), we should not let some global skepticism about the motivational powers of reason defeat proposals that aim to establish these conclusions in advance. That is, *if* it can be established that practical reason requires us to act only on, say, universalizable maxims (admittedly, a big "if"), then we would expect that this is exactly what reasonable people are motivated to do. Once we've granted that some rational considerations can motivate, it would be arbitrary to deny that others can too.

But in the absence of such a grand argument, we are left with only the plausible thought that there are some formal principles of practical reason. These principles, like the means-end principle, are not themselves grounded in desires, at least not of the ordinary sort. But they all may very well *operate* only upon pre-existing desires; for instance, if you desire something, then perhaps the means–end principle has implications for what *else* you have reason to do. So we don't yet have a cogent argument supporting the thought that there are reasons to do particular things completely in the absence of desire.

We still do have McDowell's claims about the wise person's conception of how to live—perhaps *she* acts as she does simply because she believes that doing so is right, and because of this we ordinary mortals have reasons to act in the same way. Perhaps her beliefs are intrinisically motivating and so can explain at least her own activity. But are such beliefs—or *any* beliefs—really reasons for action? And does her conception of how to live ground reasons for actions for ordinary agents?

There are reasons to be skeptical that we can understand the reasons of ordinary agents by looking to the reasons of ideal agents. First, ideal agents have reasons to do lots of things that ordinary agents do not. (Watson, 1975) points out that the flaws of ordinary people often make it unwise for them to mimic the virtuous. Suppose a defeated squash player has a very bad temper. A noble athlete would walk over to the victor right away and shake her hand, congratulating her on her victory. But a very angry defeated squash player—one who is tempted to smash his opponent's face with his racquet—has no reason to walk over to his opponent right away. Instead he has reason to first walk away and cool down. Similarly, ordinary agents can have reasons to do things that ideal agents never do. For instance, ordinary agents sometimes have reasons to take a remedial course in logic, or to go to Alcoholics Anonymous meetings. Ideal agents presumably lack such reasons.

A different sort of objection to McDowell's account is that it demands too much of ordinary agents. It might be nice if ordinary agents would instead act the way ideal agents act. No doubt this would be better in many ways. But is it really true that we are rationally *required* to act as ideal agents do? One might instead plausibly think that the reason demands something less than absolute perfection. The wise and the virtuous may not be the correct standpoint from which to understand reasons for action.

Finally, the project of grounding reasons on an ideal agent's beliefs appears to be vulnerable to a Euthyphro-style objection. Does an ideal agent have a reason to V *because* she believes that V-ing is in some way a good idea? Or does she instead believe that V-ing is in some way a good idea because she really does have a reason to V? As we shall see, suspicion that the latter way of understanding this issue is correct fuels an argument that *all* versions of psychologism are misguided.

Arguments against all forms of psychologism

WE'VE LOOKED AT some reasons for and against the thought that reasons are based on belief-desire pairs, and the thought that reasons are based on beliefs of some sort or other. But there are also grounds for thinking that psychologism of *any* form is incorrect.

Here's one such ground. It highlights the arguably rare cases when a psychological attitude *is* a reason for action. Suppose Byron wants to kill his landlord, who has been giving Byron a hard time about paying the rent late. Byron's wanting to kill his landlord is not a reason for him to buy a gun. On the contrary, buying a gun while in such a state of mind would be highly unreasonable. But his wanting to kill his landlord plausibly *is* a reason for him to seek professional counseling. Getting help to overcome his anger and malevolence makes sense. So here is an example of a psychological attitude that *does* ground a reason for action, but not in the way that psychologism pictures things. And most reasons for action *aren't* like Byron's wanting to kill his landlord.

Although this sort of argument is usually run by offering an example involving a perverse desire, we can also illustrate the argument by employing an example involving a perverse belief. Suppose Byron now believes that the United States Postal Service is out to get him. He thinks that they are spying on his every move, despite having no specific evidence that this is so. Is Byron's belief a genuine reason for him to hide from his mailman? Not really. Is his belief a reason for him to seek professional help? Most definitely. Beliefs are reasons for action when they give us some reason to get rid of them.

Examples such as these show what it is for a psychological attitude to ground a reason for action. Psychological attitudes can be reasons to act in ways to get rid of them, or to mitigate some of their perverse effects. But most reasons aren't like that; these examples are obviously unusual cases. Whether or not some psychologistic model happens to meet the Explanatory Constraint, it fails to meet the Normative Constraint. For what typically justifies action is not our beliefs about the world, but, if anything, what our beliefs are about. And so we might conclude that reasons typically are not psychological after all. The standard sort of reason is something else.

Jonathan Dancy, among others, has articulated a somewhat different argument against all psychologistic theories, an argument that also seeks to show that the belief-alone model fails to meet the Normative Constraint (2003, pp 49–60). He focuses upon moral reasons, arguing that moral reasons aren't psychological attitudes of the agent whose reasons they are, but clearly intends it to apply to other kinds of reasons for action too. Consider the following two remarks:

REASONS

(OD) Since Jodie was alone and in trouble, Mike should have offered (or, had reason to offer) help.

(SD) Since Mike believed that Jodie was alone and in trouble, Mike should have offered (or, had reason to offer) help.

We talk both ways. But when pushed, Dancy thinks that OD is canonical. Mike's reason to help Jodie is that she is in trouble. Mike's *believing* that she is in trouble is not really a reason to help her. Mike's reason, like reasons typically, is not a psychological attitude.

Things admittedly can seem otherwise. For there *is* something amiss about Mike if he falsely believes that Jodie is alone and in trouble, but fails to be motivated to offer her any help. He doesn't fail to comply with the reason mentioned in OD, because, as a matter of fact, Jodie is not alone and in trouble, and so no one, including Mike, had *that* reason to help her. And this might be taken as ground for endorsing SD instead. If Mike had a reason to help Jodie, it wasn't because she was alone and in trouble, because she in fact was not alone and in trouble. So, instead, it seems that Mike's reason to help Jodie was that *he thought* she was alone and in trouble.

There are several ways the anti-psychologist might respond. One is just to deny that Mike had any reason to help Jodie if she was not alone and in trouble. It only *seemed* to him like he had a reason. And we might want to blame him if he fails to do what it seemed to him that he had a (significant) reason to do. But this doesn't mean that he really had a reason to help her.

Dancy himself spells out another possible response. Perhaps it is true that when Jodie in fact is not in trouble, Mike does not have a reason to help her. But Mike still might have a reason to help-Jodie-when-believing-that-Jodie-is-in-trouble. That is, perhaps his reason governs a *combination* of a belief and an action, rather than just the action alone. This more complex reason directs Mike to avoid the pair of 1) refraining from helping Jodie, and 2) believing that she is in trouble. This reason permits him to do one of the two, but not both. Another way to think of it is that this reason directs Mike either 3) to not believe that Jodie is in trouble, or 4) to help her. The reason directs Mike to do at least one or the other.

This response seems unsatisfying, though. Perhaps Mike *himself* is irrational if he doesn't help Jodie when he believes that she is in trouble, but that doesn't mean that he failed to act on some *reason* he had. This supposed reason to avoid a *combination* of a belief and an action is itself neither a reason for belief nor a reason for action. It's somehow both and neither at once. It's hard to understand how we should conceive such a strange beast.

Many philosophers instead understand this sort of thing to be a *rational* requirement, rather than a *reason*. Thus we might say that Mike is rationally required either to believe that Jodie is not in trouble or to help Jodie. Mike violates this requirement if he believes that she is in trouble and does nothing to help her. He complies with this requirement either by not believing she is in trouble, or by helping her. But this requirement is not itself a reason. After all, this requirement might govern Mike without him having a reason to do or believe anything in particular.

The relation between reasons and rational requirements, whatever it is, is very complex, and is currently the focus of much philosophical activity. We don't have space here to explore this relation; it would take another monograph to investigate the relationship *between* reasons and rationality. Instead, at the end of the book I point the reader to some good starting points for understanding this relation.

Dancy's argument here is intended to bring out how awkward it is to say that a (moral) reason for action such as Mike's is a psychological state of Mike's. Mike's reason to help isn't grounded upon what Mike thinks or wants; rather, it has something to do with the situation that Mike faces. But this "something" is unsatisfactorily vague. And so in the next chapter we will investigate Dancy's and others' proposed *solutions* to understanding what reasons such as Mike's might be.

CHAPTER FOUR

Deontic, value-based, and primitivist accounts

Factualism

SO PERHAPS REASONS aren't thoughts, wants, or anything else psychological. Psychologism of any variety seems not to meet the Normative Constraint in particular. But what are our alternatives?

One is to think that reasons are facts, truths, propositions, or states of affairs—although there are subtle metaphysical differences among these various disjuncts that we can set aside for now. The following thoughts all seem rather natural. The reason to quit smoking is that smoking causes cancer. My reason for driving to school is that my daughter is there waiting for me. Your reason for reading this chapter might be that it investigates whether reasons are facts. In these examples, none of the reasons mentioned are psychological attitudes.

We do often talk this way. Ordinary language commonly identifies reasons with facts or propositions. Call the philosophical theory of reasons that aims to vindicate this bit of ordinary language *factualism*. According to the simplest version of factualism, all reasons are facts. What reason is there to climb Mt.

Everest? Because it's there! Not: because I believe it's there. Nor: because I want to climb it. According to factualism, Mallory had it right.

But linguistic evidence hardly settles the issue. Even though we commonly characterize reasons as facts, we characterize them as psychological with comparable frequency. This is especially likely when the speaker fails to share the perspective of the agent about whom she speaks. While *I* would tell you that my reason for going to the concert tonight is that Sonic Youth will be playing dissonant music there, someone who doesn't care for dissonant music would be very likely to characterize my reason for going to the concert in psychological terms: Eric *wants* to hear dissonant music. Such a person would be inclined to put the reason that way because she herself does not take the fact that Sonic Youth is playing dissonant music as any reason whatsoever to go. Something similar occurs when the speaker does not believe what the agent believes: a skeptic about the efficacy of vaccines would not characterize your reason for getting the flu shot in the same way that you would. So speakers often resort to psychological language when there are relevant differences between the perspective of the speaker and that of the agent. We must look beyond data from ordinary language in order to make real progress.

The best reason for thinking that reasons are facts is that facts of a certain sort, unlike psychological attitudes, seem to be able to meet the Normative Constraint. But even then there remains the question of what *kind* of facts reasons are. The quickest fix understands reasons to be *inherently* normative, or that they are constituted by something else inherently normative. There are several different ways that factualists develop this idea. Here we will sketch a few.

Primitivism

SOME ARGUE THAT the concept of a reason is the primary normative concept. Our grasp of normativity itself comes through our grasp of what a reason is. We cannot explain the normativity of reasons by attempting to reduce reasons to something *else*. As we saw in Chapter 1, Tim Scanlon opens his book by embracing this view:

I will take the idea of a reason as primitive. Any attempt to explain what it is to be a reason for something seems to me to lead back to the same idea: a consideration that counts in favour of it. "Counts in favour how?" one might ask. "By providing a reason for it" seems to be the only answer. (1998, p 17)

Derek Parfit likewise says in the first chapter of his new book:

It is hard to explain the *concept* of a reason, or what the phrase "a reason" means. Facts give us reasons, we might say, when they count in favour of our having some attitude, or our acting in some way. But "counting in favour of" means roughly "gives a reason for". Like some other fundamental concepts, such as those involved in our thoughts about time, consciousness, and possibility, the concept of a reason is indefinable in the sense that it cannot be helpfully explained merely by using other words. We must explain such concepts in a different way, by getting people to think thoughts that use these concepts. (2011, p 31)

Parfit calls this a *nonreductive* theory of reasons, since he thinks that the concept of a reason cannot be reduced to other concepts. To put this idea positively, we might characterize it instead as *primitivism*, since it regards the concept of a reason to be fundamental or primitive.

Some primitivists think that the concept of a reason explains other evaluative and normative concepts. For example, perhaps the concept of ought is based upon the concept of a reason, the thought being that you ought to V simply because you have most reason to V. Or, as "buck-passers" maintain, perhaps the concept of good is based upon the concept of a reason, the thought being that some A is good simply because you have reason to respond to A in some positive way. Then again, one might be a primitivist about reasons without any ambition to reduce other evaluative and normative concepts to the concept of a reason; one could hold that there are multiple independent fundamental normative concepts here.

Let's set those debates aside, and focus instead upon the core thesis of primitivism. It's a thesis that seems difficult to prove. For if we had a theory of reasons that successfully grounded the concept of a reason upon some other concept(s), then we would have an theory *dis*proving primitivism. But the best support for primitivism seems to be the *absence* of any such argument. So we must consider the merits of alternative conceptions of reasons.

Reasons as explanations of ought-facts

A SECOND STRATEGY explains the concept of a reason in terms of other normative concepts. Perhaps the concept of a reason isn't itself directly normative, but gets its normativity from its relation to other inherently normative concepts. The most likely candidate concept might be the concept of "ought." The thought here is that the concept of 'ought' is more fundamental than that of a reason. Perhaps reasons can even be partially reduced to or defined in terms of the concept of "ought."

Start with the idea that there are things you ought to do. For instance, those in Glasgow ought to carry an umbrella. Presumably, there is some reason you ought to do this, perhaps even more than one reason. But what does it mean to say that you have a reason to carry an umbrella in Glasgow? Does it mean anything other than that you *ought* to do so?

One clear difference between reasons and oughts is that you can have a reason to do things that you ought not do. You may have a reason (or some reason) to cheat on your tax return. But you shouldn't do it. Reasons seem normatively lighter or weaker than oughts.

We can begin to make sense of this difference by noting you can have a reason to do something, and yet have a better reason (or, perhaps, more reasons) *not* to do it, or to do something that is an alternative to it. Even though you have some sort of reason to cheat on your taxes, you probably have better reason(s) to complete your return accurately. A reason that can be overruled or outweighed in this way is sometimes called a *pro tanto reason*. You can have a pro tanto reason to cheat on your taxes even though you ought not to. Your reason to do what you ought to do—here, to complete your tax return accurately—is sometimes called a *perfect reason*. Oughts and perfect reasons are verdictive or decisive, whereas pro tanto reasons need not be.

So that's one difference between some reasons and oughts. Another difference is that you can have multiple reasons to complete your tax return accurately, but it isn't obvious that you can't have multiple oughts to complete your return accurately. Reasons are thus somewhat different from oughts. How should we understand all this?

John Broome (2004) has argued that reasons for action *explain why* you ought to do things. A reason for you to V is thus part of an explanation why you ought to V. Reasons are what they are because they help explain why people ought to do certain things or why people ought to believe certain things.

We can see how Broome's view has room to accommodate the idea that one can have multiple reasons for doing something. The full explanation for why you ought to do something can be complex, and each part of the explanation can be one of the multiple reasons to do it. The multiple reasons, when put all together, fully explain why you ought to do it. So Broome has no problem making sense of the idea that you can have several distinct reasons for doing what you ought to do.

Let's now look at the difference between perfect reasons and pro tanto reasons. Broome's argument seems to account most naturally for perfect reasons. A perfect reason for you to V explains why you ought to V. But sometimes you have a pro tanto reason to V in a circumstance in which you ought *not* to V. Such a reason can hardly explain why you ought to V, because it just *isn't* true that you ought to V. If pro tanto reasons cannot be understood as explanations of ought-facts in this way, we might wonder how Broome *can* account for them.

His solution is complex. He still tries to relate pro tanto reasons to explanations of ought-facts. To do so, he conceives of each pro tanto reason as having a weight attached to it, a weight indicating how important it is. Suppose the fact that cheating on your taxes would save you some money is a pro tanto reason to cheat on your taxes. And suppose the fact that it would be illegal to cheat on your taxes is a pro tanto reason not to cheat on your taxes. The first reason is a reason for cheating; the second is a reason against cheating. Now suppose further that you ought not cheat on your taxes. Broome thinks that each of the reasons plays a role in explaining why you ought not cheat: the weight of the reason for cheating is greater than the weight of the reason against cheating. So, what explains why you ought not to cheat? The reasons, and their weight. Even the reason *for* cheating plays a role in explaining why you ought *not* to cheat here and now, because such a reason also plays a role in explaining why, if there were *other* weighty reasons for cheating, it would then be true that you ought to cheat. The weight of this pro tanto reason would be part of the story. Pro tanto reasons, then, turn out to be facts that plays this characteristic role in a weighing explanation. Even pro tanto reasons, then, can be captured by Broome's analysis.

So on Broome's view, a reason is different from but related to an ought-fact. The concept of reason is to be understood in terms of two concepts that are more fundamental: the concept of 'ought' and the concept of explanation. A reason for you to do something is nothing but part of what explains why you ought to do it.

Broome's account thus displays how reasons have both an explanatory and a normative role. They have an explanatory role because they help explain why you ought to do things. And they are normative in that they reveal why certain normative truths (ought-facts) are as they are.

Reasons as evidence

A THIRD STRATEGY also forges a conceptual link between reasons and ought-facts. Perhaps, however, the relation is not the specific link Broome holds. Instead of thinking that reasons *explain* ought-facts, we might think that reasons are *evidence* of ought-facts. The idea here is that some consideration is reason for you to V just in case it is evidence that you ought to V. (In fact, this analysis applies not only to reasons for action, but to reasons for belief as well: a reason to believe p is just evidence that you ought to believe p.) For instance, the fact that smoking causes cancer is both a reason for a smoker to quit smoking and is evidence that she ought to quit smoking. Perhaps the best explanation of this coincidence is just that reasons and evidence are conceptually linked.

This view is proposed by Kearns and Star (2008; 2009). They characterize their *reasons-as-evidence view* this way:

> Necessarily, a fact F is a reason for an agent A to φ if and only if F is evidence that A ought to φ (where φ is either a belief or an action). (2009, p 216)

Reasons are facts that explain why we ought to act and believe as we should.

Kearns and Star give several different arguments for thinking that the reasons-as-evidence view is true. Here, very briefly, are a few of these arguments. First, they argue that the reasons-as-evidence view promises to provide a unified account of reasons, since it at once accounts for both reasons for belief and reasons for action. (Note that Broome can say the same of his own view.) Second, evidence that A ought to V seems to play the same roles in deliberation and in convincing others that reasons for V-ing play. Third, the reasons-as-evidence view has the best account for the fact that reasons have different weights, their weights being proportional to their evidential value. Strong reasons for V-ing are also strong evidence that one ought to V. So while Broome argues that reasons are explanations of ought-facts, Star and Kearns argue that reasons are evidence of ought-facts.

Should we prefer the reasons-as-evidence view to Broome's reasons-as-explanation view? (Kearns and Star, 2008) argue that we should. They hold that some reasons are not explanations but are evidence that one ought to do something. Consider a piece of *undiscovered* evidence. That evidence can be a reason for you to believe that which it is evidence for, even though—as long as it remains undiscovered—it isn't any part of an explanation concerning what you ought to believe. For example, suppose there has been a murder and that Bob's fingerprints are on the murder weapon. The fingerprints are a reason for you to believe that Bob is the murderer. But no one has recovered the weapon yet. And as long as it remains undiscovered, the fingerprints do not *explain* why you ought to believe that Bob is the murderer. Indeed, they can't explain why you ought to believe that Bob is the murderer, because until you have epistemic access to the fingerprints, it isn't really true that you ought to believe that Bob is the murderer. But all hidden away, the fingerprints remain evidence. Evidence can be unavailable. And these unavailable fingerprints are evidence that you ought to believe that Bob is the murderer, even if you never discover it, and even if you never are aware of this reason. You may not *have* this reason to believe that Bob is the murderer until you are aware of it, but even so there still *is* a reason for you to believe that Bob is the murderer. So reasons and evidence-of-oughts seem to go together.[1]

The tight connection between *reasons* and *ought* championed both by Broome and by Star and Kearns has been challenged.

Dancy argues that not all reasons for action ground conclusions about what one ought to do. Some reasons are instead *enticing reasons*. He writes,

> Enticing reasons are to do with what would be fun, amusing, attractive, exciting, pleasant and so on. They can be stronger and weaker, and they are often strong enough for action. But (as I understand the matter) they never take us to an ought; it is not true of an enticing reason that if one has one of them and no reason of any other sort, one ought to do what the reason entices one to do. One can do that; but one has the right not to. (Dancy, 2006, p 43)

The idea here is that some reasons merely count in favor of the actions for which they are reasons, without ever making it true that one ought to so act. Not all reasons normatively compel action. Anscombe seemed to have much the same idea in mind:

> It is obvious that I can decide, on general grounds about colouring and so on, that a certain dress in a shop window would suit me very well, without its following that I can be accused of some kind of inconsistency with what I have decided if I do not thereupon go in and buy it; even if there are no impediments, such as shortage of cash, at all. (Anscombe, 2000, p 59)

A different but related idea is that some reasons are merely supererogatory. You have a reason of some sort, I suppose, to learn Assyrian, or to wash your neighbor's car. But even if there are no reasons not to so act, it isn't really true that you *ought* to anyway. That seems much too severe. To say that you ought to learn Assyrian is thus to say something stronger than that you have a reason to do so and no reason not to.

Enticing reasons, and perhaps also supererogatory reasons, thus seem not to be related to oughts in the way that other reasons are. So, if this points to a failure of any view of reasons based around oughts, is there a better way to account for the normative dimension of reasons for action?

Reasons as indicators of value

A FOURTH STRATEGY explains the concept of a reason in terms of *evaluative* concepts. At its most basic, the thought here is that you have reason to V just in case your V-ing would be *good* in some way. The normativity of reasons is thus accounted for by the goodness of the actions for which you have reasons.

Joseph Raz (1999, pp 22–3) writes that "[v]aluable aspects of the world constitute reasons ..." Acting for a reason, on this view, is acting for a fact in virtue of which the action is good in some way or other. When I recycle my empty plastic bottle for a reason, I recycle it in virtue of some good aspect of recycling it. To recycle for a reason is to recycle for some point or purpose in light of which I might be motivated to recycle. For example, I might recycle it so that it won't end up in a landfill, or so that others will think well of me. Either of these two good aspects of recycling makes my recycling intelligible. Without *some* such good aspect of recycling in view, I won't be recycling the plastic bottle for a reason.

On this view, facts about what's good are the source of reasons for action. And if this view is right, then it appears to be very clear how reasons justify the actions that they are reasons for: they do so because of the supposed conceptual connexion between reasons and the good. To put the idea Platonically, Reason itself depends upon the Form of the Good. So say these *evaluativists*.

One clear advantage of evaluativism is that it makes room for enticing reasons. That there is some good aspect to acting in a particular way gives you some reason to so act, without it thereby being true that you *ought* to so act. Reasons are normatively weaker than oughts, so connecting reasons with goodness avoids the problem Dancy highlights.

One might worry, however, that goodness is *too* weak to meet the Normative Constraint. Perhaps there are many good aspects of acting in some particular way that give you no reason whatsoever so to act, not even a tiny enticing reason. Calling a foul on a particular football player might please the crowd, surely a good thing. But this good thing plausibly gives the referee no reason to call a foul on the player. The evaluativist will need to say something about how we are to exclude cases like these. And there are other challenges to evaluativism, challenges it shares with the other forms of factualism mentioned so far. Let's take up these challenges next.

The challenge to factualism

WE SEE FOUR different ways of understanding reasons to be not psychological attitudes, but as some fact necessarily constituted by or related to some sort of value. In the remainder of this chapter, we will focus on the advantages and disadvantages that these various factualist strategies collectively share.

Factualism (no matter what the variety) appears most plausible when we recall the importance of the Normative Requirement. You have a reason to recycle your empty plastic bottles, and this reason shows why so acting is justified: doing so harms the environment and future generations less than sending them to the landfill does. And this is a reason whether you care about the environment and future generations or not, whether you believe that recycling benefits the environment or not.

Even if reasons so understood are essentially normative, they however are not always *explicitly* normative. Despite the differences flagged above, all of the theories on display here conceive of reasons as garden-variety facts. For instance, they agree that my reason to go to the Sonic Youth show might be something like the fact that Sonic Youth will be playing dissonant music, a fact that does not *explicitly* mention any "oughts" or "goods."

But they would disagree with each other about *why* this garden-variety fact is indeed a reason. Broome would say that this fact is a reason to go to the show because it explains why I ought to go to the show. Kearns and Star would instead say it's because this fact is evidence that I ought to go to the show. Evaluativists would say that this fact is a reason because the goodness of going to the show constitutes the reason to go to the show. And primitivists would say that we cannot further explain why this fact is a reason to go to the show; it just *is* such a reason, which is inherently normative.

All these factualists, then, see reasons to be necessarily related to the good or the normative. So factualism is well-suited to meet the Normative Requirement. But it is precisely to the same extent ill-suited to meet the Explanatory Requirement. Recall that reasons can potentially explain the actions that they are reasons for. If you have a reason to stop by the office over the weekend, it is possible for you to stop by the office *for* that reason. But if reasons are just facts, not constituted out of the agent's psychology, then it is far from clear how reasons so understood could themselves explain action. How can facts alone do *that*? Facts appear to be too impersonal—too unagential—to be the sort of thing that could explain rational action.

This allegation, however, is not itself an argument against the factualist; rather, it prompts us to look for one.

The argument from error

CONSIDER, THEN, AN argument challenging the explanatory power of factualism that we might call the argument from error. Return to our previous example. Suppose you go to a Sonic Youth concert because Sonic Youth is playing dissonant music. Davidson and others will insist that your fully specified reason for action is that you *want* to listen to something dissonant, and you *believe* that attending the Sonic Youth concert would count as listening to something dissonant. That is, they hold that the "Sonic Youth plays dissonant music" expression in our original explanation, as the factualist would have it, is really just shorthand for the actual reason: the belief/pro-attitude pair.

Now one reason for insisting this is that the belief/pro-attitude pair would have been your reason for going to the Sonic Youth concert even if Sonic Youth were not playing dissonant music— perhaps, unbeknown to you, they're weary of dissonance, and are now playing only major chord surf-pop melodies. You are likely to be disappointed! But it would seem a mistake, it appears, to say that you are going to a Sonic Youth concert for the reason that they are playing dissonant music, because they just *aren't* playing dissonant music. The explanans in any plausible explanation, it seems, must be true. (Later, we will see that this can be challenged.) And it *isn't* true that Sonic Youth is playing dissonant music at the concert to which you go. So that, it seems, can't really be your reason for going. Instead, your reason, at least in this case, very much seems to be your belief/pro-attitude pair. That's the first step of the argument: that in the case where you are wrong about things, what explains your action is your psychology.

The second step of the argument extrapolates from the case of error. This step says that the form of an action-explanation does not depend upon whether the agent is in error. The same form of explanation that works in the case of error should also work in the case where there is no error (Williams, 1981, p 102). Whether what you believe is true or false doesn't affect the form of the explanation of what you do. So if you going to the Sonic Youth show is explained by your psychological attitudes in the case where you *falsely* believe that Sonic Youth will be playing dissonant music, then you going to the Sonic Youth show is also explained by your psychological attitudes in the case where you *truly* believe that Sonic Youth will be playing dissonant music. In every case, then, psychological attitudes explain action. Hence the Argument from Error.

The Argument from Error is structurally similar to the Argument from Illusion in epistemology. There it is argued that all we know are appearances, or *sense-data*. After all, sometimes we see things that aren't really there (or *out* there). When we are under an illusion, what we *are* directly aware of, it seems, are sense data. But if we are directly aware of sense data when we are under an illusion, and if the kind of thing of which we aware is the same whether or not we are under an illusion, then we are directly aware only of sense data, even when we are not under an illusion.

The Argument from Illusion has fallen out of fashion in epistemology. There are several different lines of objection to it. But the most well known opponents are the disjunctivists. Disjunctivists deny that there must be some common kind in cases of both error and veridicality. What Penny sees when she thinks she is seeing an oasis need not be of the same ontological category in the case where she gets it correct as it is when she is merely seeing a mirage. No doubt, Penny herself will not always be in a position to determine whether she is under an illusion, or whether she is seeing things as they are. But the disjunctivist insists that her inability to determine which of these two possibilities are realized does not mean that she is in fact directly aware only of sense data in the case where there is no illusion. Rather, in the case where Penny gets things right, she really sees an oasis, not just an appearance of an oasis. There is no reason to insist that the two cases must be treated alike.

Now let's turn from epistemology to action. The *practical* disjunctivist can concede that in the case where you are wrong about whether Sonic Youth will be playing dissonant music at the concert you plan to attend, your going may very well be explained by your psychological attitudes: your wanting to hear dissonant music and your conviction that Sonic Youth will be playing dissonant music. But the practical disjunctivist resists the urge to generalize from the case of error. In the case where you are under no error, you are going to a Sonic Youth concert because Sonic Youth is playing dissonant music. Of course, you yourself won't always be able to discern which of these two possibilities are realized. But this does not mean that your reasons are based upon psychological attitudes in the case where you are making no error. In the case where you get things right, you go to the concert because Sonic Youth is playing dissonant music, not just because you think they are. *Pace* Williams, we should not insist that the two cases must be treated alike.

The disjunctivist, even if successful, does concede something to the defender of psychologism. If disjunctivism is correct, then standard reasons for action may well be facts. But in cases of error, reasons remain psychological. So disjunctivism does not vindicate factualism entirely. At best, it vindicates the factualist interpretation of only most reasons for action.

This disjunctivist response to the Argument from Error is now well known. But there are additional reasons for resisting the Argument from Error. That argument seems persuasive largely because it focuses your attention on the fact that you might be wrong about whether, e.g. Sonic Youth is playing dissonant music. Since you could be wrong about that, it can seem that that can't be your reason even in cases in which you are not wrong. The unexpressed premise in the Argument from Error seems to be that while you can be wrong about whether Sonic Youth is playing dissonant music, you can't be wrong about whether you think they are, nor about whether you want to hear dissonant music. Error, it is supposed, is a possibility only about the way the world is, not about your own psychology.

But once this premise is articulated, its plausibility dissipates. Of course you can be wrong about what you believe. You can also be wrong about what you want. It may be granted that there are cases where you really do think Sonic Youth will be playing dissonant music and you really do want to hear some dissonant music, and this belief/pro-attitude pair causes you to head to the concert. But you might also head off to the concert in the case where, for example, you *think* you want to hear some dissonant music, and yet really you don't. Still, your *thought* that you want to hear some dissonant music might cause you to go, just as in the more ordinary case your *wanting* to hear some dissonant music might cause you to go. The kinds of explanations involved in these two cases differ: in one case, the explanans is a first-order psychological attitude, while in the other case the explanans is a second-order psychological attitude. This is possible even if you yourself are unable to discern which of these two possibilities is realized.

Now, we can imagine someone insisting that since you *could* be wrong about whether your first-order psychological attitudes explain your action, then it must follow that they never explain your action, on the grounds that we must suppose that the same form of explanation applies in both cases. Such a person is insisting that second-order psychological attitudes are the explanantia in *every* case.

But this is not persuasive. Allowing that there can be rare cases in which second-order psychological attitudes are indeed the relevant explanantia does not force us to grant that such attitudes explain in every case. Sometimes, weird cases are ... well, weird. A second reason not to be moved by this argument is that to accept it would lead to regress problems. After all, just as we aren't omniscient about our first-order psychological attitudes, so too are we not omniscient about our second-order psychological attitudes. It would take more work to concoct an example in which one's mistaken second-order psychological attitude explains one's action. But clever philosophers could produce one, no doubt. And so even second-order psychological attitudes do not provide us with the kind of epistemic bedrock on which to launch any argument that insists that all action explanations must be of the same form.

Nor can we find that bedrock (or heaven?) by ascending still higher. There's no good reason to think that we are omniscient about any nth-order psychological attitude. Error is always possible. And so *if* the possibility of error about the world (such as whether Sonic Youth is playing dissonant music) rules out any and all explanations of action by reference to the world itself, then the possibility of error about our own minds rules out any and all explanation of action by reference to any nth-order psychological attitude as well. But where would that leave us? If neither the world nor our minds were to explain action, then what would? Thus we shouldn't insist that the correct rational explanation of action will be of the same kind or form in each and every case. Perhaps our actions are to be explained sometimes in one way; sometimes another. The Argument from Error, as so far articulated, doesn't show that factualism is false.[2]

There may still be a better version of the Argument from Error available, a version that does not rely upon whether our knowledge of our own psychological life is infallible. A more promising approach would not rely on the idea that we are sometimes mistaken, but upon the idea that it does not matter whether we are mistaken.[3] I leave it to others more sympathetic to the conclusion to develop this line of argument.

Dancy

ONE MAY STILL have the nagging sense that reasons can't be mind-independent facts, simply because they cannot explain all the actions for which they are reasons. Such facts don't seem to be the right sort of ontological beast to do the kind of explanatory work reasons do. Even if the Argument from Error isn't the correct way to bring out this worry, skepticism seems to be especially severe in cases where agents who act for reasons are mistaken about relevant facts.

But Dancy has proposed a way out. He argues that action explanations need not be factive. That is, he argues that the thing that explains action need not actually be true in order to explain. As a result, you can act for a reason that isn't a psychological attitude of yours even in the case where you are mistaken about the facts.

This idea is best understood by considering an example. The defender of psychologism might explain your action this way:

> Your reason for going to the Sonic Youth show is that you believe they will be playing dissonant music there.

The defender of factualism might instead explain your action this way:

Your reason for going to the Sonic Youth show is that they will
be playing dissonant music there.

The two proposed explanations are very different, but they have
in common the feature that the purported explanans (the clause
coming after the "is that") is true. The first explanation works only
if you really do believe that Sonic Youth will be playing dissonant
music at the show. Likewise, the second explanation works only if
Sonic Youth really will be playing dissonant music at the show. But
if either explanans is false, the proposed explanations fail.

Dancy, however, proposes a different sort of explanation. We
might instead explain your action as follows:

Your reason for going to the Sonic Youth show is that they will
be playing dissonant music there, as you believe.

Here your action is explained by the consideration that Sonic
Youth will be playing dissonant music there, which is something
you believe. This consideration wouldn't motivate you if you didn't
believe it; but your reason isn't your belief, but instead it's *what*
you believe. Your reason is much the same thing that the factualist
says it is, but it turns out that it doesn't have to be true in order for
you to act on it as a reason. Even if it's false that Sonic Youth was
playing dissonant music there, we still might say that you went to
the Sonic Youth show because, as you believed, they were playing
dissonant music there. The explanans does not have to be true in
order to explain your action. Explanations need not be factive. So
Dancy is, in a sense, a non-factive factualist.

Dancy admits that his proposal sounds odd. There appears to
be something counterintuitive about non-factive explanations. But
Dancy notes that we do talk this way sometimes. For instance,
suppose that one day we discover that Governor George Ryan of
Illinois did not actually commit racketeering or fraud, as the Court
ruled. If someone asks us why Ryan was imprisoned, we still might
correctly say that he was sentenced to six and a half years in prison
for racketeering and fraud. Those *were* the crimes for which he
was convicted and imprisoned, after all. And we can say this even
if we think that Ryan did not commit fraud or engage in a racket.
To explain that he was imprisoned for fraud and racketeering is
not necessarily to endorse the soundness of the Court's ruling. This

explanation of why the Court sentenced him need not be construed factively. Why was he put in prison? For committing fraud and racketeering.

If correct, we should not be opposed in principle to non-factive explanations. Sometimes, they work. There's no doubt that when you explain something, you *pragmatically* imply that the explanans is indeed true. If in the above situation you explain to someone that Governor Ryan was imprisoned for racketeering and fraud, it would be rude not to add that (you think) he didn't really commit these crimes. Adding this, however, would not take back what you originally said. So this shows that the original explanation, though perhaps misleading, is not incorrect. Non-factive explanations are indeed possible.

If this is right, then we have the ingredients necessary for meeting the Explanatory and the Normative Constraints at once. The Normative Constraint can naturally be met because considerations, rather than beliefs about considerations, themselves justify actions. Your reason for helping your friend is not that you *believe* she needs help, but that she indeed needs it. On the other hand, in order to meet the Explanatory Constraint, it seems we must allow for the fact that you can do things for reasons even when you don't have the facts right. Dancy's proposal accomplishes this, since considerations putatively explain actions even when they don't obtain. The same action rationalization works no matter whether the agent's beliefs are true. So if we are happy with the idea of non-factive explanations, then Dancy's proposal meets the Explanatory Constraint too.

But that is a big "if." Many find that while that the occasional non-factive explanation makes sense, such explanations are at best incomplete or shorthand, and should instead canonically be expressed (and people part ways here) either as factualists recommend or as psychologists recommend, rather than by some awkward amalgam of the two. The idea that something that isn't the case can explain something that *is* the case is a bitter pill to swallow.

Dancy concedes that the idea that there are non-factive *causal* explanations is implausible (2003, p 161). If one thing or fact causes another, they both of course must obtain or somehow be real. But Dancy thinks that reasons explanations aren't a form of causal explanation. He prefers to construe reasons explanation with the "in the light of" locution. For instance, I might go to the Sonic Youth show in the light of the consideration that you will be there, and not in the light of the consideration that they will be playing dissonant music. And this is true even if you won't in fact be there. I can go to the show in the light of some consideration that (unbeknown to me) doesn't obtain.

This much seems true. But the "in the light of" locution seems awfully metaphorical. Considerations don't really shine light, *especially* if they don't obtain. Accounting for reasons in this way amounts to accounting for the obscure in terms of the even more obscure. It seems as though Dancy really wants to be a hardcore factualist, and tries to get a close to factualism as one can while still aiming to pay homage to the Explanatory Constraint.

Of course, it's easy to register dissatisfaction with his and others' efforts. But to make progress, we must not merely note our dissatisfaction. We must express it as best we can in order to figure how to do better.

Factualism, the explanatory requirement, and agency

HERE'S ONE WAY to express this dissatisfaction. Factualism bears a complex relation to the agent's own perspective upon her reasons for action. If you are grading student papers, you are unlikely to express your reasons for doing so in terms of what you think and want. You are grading their papers—you might say—because you are the instructor. It would be odd to instead say that you are grading their papers because *you believe* that you are the instructor. It would be similarly odd to say that you are grading their papers because *you want* to do your job, instead of saying, more straightforwardly, because it's your job. Agents typically conceive of their reasons not in terms of their own psychological attitudes, but in terms of the facts. On this score, factualism seems to do more justice to the agent's own perspective than psychologism does.

Yet there is still a sense in which factualism fails to capture the *practical* perspective that the agent takes toward her reasons. Factualists tend to offer up examples like the following in order to bolster their position:

It seems to me, however, blatantly obvious that most of our moral duties [and reasons] are grounded in features of the situation, not in our beliefs about how things are. It is because she is in trouble that I ought to help her, not because I think she is in trouble. What made it wrong for her to behave in this way was that she had promised not to, not that she believed she had promised not to. What made it wrong for him not to turn up was that it made it impossible for her to get home that evening. The reason why I should go and see my sister is that she has been ill. And so on. (Dancy, 2003, p 52)

The features of the situation that supposedly ground an agent's reasons (moral and perhaps otherwise) are indeed what an agent focuses upon when deliberating. But the features of the situation that the agent faces still capture only part of the agential perspective. I might initially say that the reason why I should see my sister is that she has been ill, but this response is incomplete. My sister's illness is a reason for me to see her only if such a visit would do her some good. If my sister hates me, visiting her while she is sick will probably make her even more miserable. Seeing her when she is ill makes sense only if I will be welcome. (If the illness afflicting my sister is extremely contagious, then visiting her while she is sick is also probably a very bad idea.)

Dancy explicitly acknowledges that a fact (such as, my sister has been ill) that is a reason for me to do something (visit her) is not necessarily generalizable: not everyone who has an ill sister has a reason to visit her. Considerations that normally are reasons can be undercut by other considerations (such as, my sister hates me). What is a reason here and now might not be a reason in different circumstances.

Recognizing the existence of undercutting reasons goes some way toward capturing what's special about the agent's perspective, for what's true of one agent isn't thereby true of all. But acknowledging undercutting reasons still does not suffice to capture the practical nature of practical reasons.

The fact that my sister has been ill is relevant to the question whether I have a reason to visit her simply because in visiting her, I would thereby be (say) comforting her, making her feel better, and/or helping her pass the time. The fact that she is sick means (among other things) that I can *do* something by visiting her that

I would not be doing if I were instead visiting a healthy or hostile sibling. My action-options when my sister is ill differ from my action-options when she is healthy. Now, we often need to say only things like "My sister has been ill" in order to convey the reason for visiting. People typically need not be *told* that the ill tend to feel comforted by the presence and attention of their loved ones, and that such comfort can even aid recovery. But it's because of such facts that we have a special reason to visit our ill relatives. In the absence of the possibility of comforting my sister, helping her pass the time, etc., it's not obvious how the fact that my sister has been ill is even relevant to the question why I am going to see her. Her illness matters only because I can thereby do things that I wouldn't be in a position to do otherwise.

So factualists aren't wrong to think that the perspective of agency puts facts rather than the agent's own state of mind front and centre. But these facts are themselves relevant only as far as they shape the practical possibilities agents face. We can revisit some of Dancy's examples with this point in mind. He is of course correct to say that "it is because she is in trouble that I ought to help her, not because I think she is in trouble ..." But her being in trouble makes it possible for me to do something—help her—that I would be unable to do if she were entirely self-sufficient. The fact that she is in trouble is practically relevant because it makes it possible for me to help her. If she weren't in trouble, I wouldn't be able to help her. I'd just get in her way.

Dancy is likewise correct to say that "what made it wrong for her to behave in this way was that she had promised not to [behave in this way], not that she believed she had promised not to." The fact that she promised not to do something is practically relevant to her reason not to do it. But this fact is relevant only because she would thereby be breaking a promise if she did what she promised that she wouldn't do. She could say "I'm not behaving that way, for the reason that I'm thereby keeping my promise."

These considerations indicate that facts that float completely free of our agency aren't reasons; rather, they are relevant because they shape what we can do. The fact that my sister is ill means that I now can, among other things, distract her from her discomfort. The fact that I promised to do something means that I now can keep or break my promise. The fact that she needs help means that I now can help her. These facts are related to reasons, because they help constitute our practical options.

So facts by themselves seem not to be reasons for action. Reasons for actions are inherently more practical than that. In the final chapter, I'll show how we might build a rival account of reasons for action out of this observation. But first we should investigate what's now the most popular view of reasons for action, the view that there are multiple kinds of reasons.

CHAPTER FIVE

Hybrid theories

We have seen that psychologistic theories of reasons seem fairly well suited to meeting the Explanatory Constraint, but have trouble when it comes to meeting the Normative Constraint. We have also seen that factualist theories of reasons seem fairly well suited to meeting the Normative Constraint, but have trouble when it comes to meeting the Explanatory Constraint.

In light of this, many if not most philosophers now respond to this problem by distinguishing two different kinds of reasons, each of which meets one but not the other constraint. Motivating reasons (sometimes called explanatory reasons) are the reasons we act for; normative reasons (sometimes called justifying reasons) are the reasons that make so acting the thing to do. The strategy is that we can meet all the relevant Constraints by distinguishing between these two different types of reasons.

Building normative reasons out of motivating reasons

ONE OF THE most ambitious and sophisticated attempts to reconcile psychologism with the Justificatory Constraint can be found in the work of Michael Smith. Smith aims to offer us a roughly Humean theory of the motivational power of reasons that *also* yields (among other things) the intuitive result that the Heartless Husband has a reason to treat his wife well. While Smith's view of the nature of reasons is complex and systematic, we can canvass several of its more distinctive features that go some way toward producing a theory that meets the various desiderata any successful account of reasons should satisfy.

The linchpin of Smith's view is a distinction he draws between two different kinds of reason. Smith clearly demarcates motivating reasons and normative reasons. *Motivating reasons* are the reasons constituted by an appropriately paired belief and "desire" (or pro-attitude). Motivating reasons are well-suited to explain action, for they are psychologically real. Whenever someone does something for a reason, the reason in question is a motivating reason.

Normative reasons, however, are very different. Normative reasons, according to Smith, are truths of the form of V-ing is required by some normative system. To say that you have a normative reason to V is to say that you are under a normative requirement to V, a requirement that stems from some normative system that applies to you. Normative reasons, which are just normative facts of a certain sort then, seem well suited to justify the actions for which they are reasons. The Heartless Husband may have no motivating reason to be nicer to his wife, but he still has a normative reason to do so. By distinguishing motivating reasons from normative reasons, Smith can call upon each to satisfy two of our several Constraints as appropriate. Motivating reasons satisfy the Explanatory Constraint, while normative reasons satisfy the Normative Constraint.

The distinction between motivating reasons and normative reasons is now enormously popular among philosophers who work in the area. It is common to take it for granted that normative reasons and motivating reasons are just different beasts.

But not everyone agrees that the distinction between motivating reasons and normative reasons is itself well motivated (or justified). Others insist that the reasons that motivate you must be identical to the reasons that potentially make your action correct or justified. On this view, while there are surely reasons that explain but not justify, and reasons that justify but not explain, reasons *can* also do both. Sometimes you are motivated by the reasons that make your action reasonable to do.

Here is another way to put the worry about Smith's distinction. Davidson and Williams both held that the reasons that explain action can also, to at least some extent, justify action. Reasons have both an explanatory and a justificatory dimension. The problem with their views seemed to be that their conception of reasons, in attempting to account for the explanatory or motivational power of reasons, fails to *adequately* account for the normative or justificatory power of reasons: recall the case of the Heartless Husband. Of course, Williams consciously chose to accept this conclusion, arguing that if the Heartless Husband has no internal reason to be nicer to his wife, then he has no reason of any sort. But by helping himself to the notion of a non-psychological reason, Smith might appear to be merely assuming the existence of what Williams and many others deny. So we need to see whether and why Smith is entitled to posit normative reasons that are distinct from the reasons that motivate us.

Now Smith too acknowledges that reasons have both an explanatory and a justificatory dimension. But he denies that all reasons must potentially both explain and justify that for which they are reasons. Rather, only motivating reasons directly explain, and only normative reasons primarily justify. So why, then, call both *reasons*? He offers two answers.

Smith (1987) first held that both motivating reasons and normative reasons do indeed justify the actions that they are reasons for, but they justify in very different ways. Normative reasons, which have no explanatory role, justify actions from the perspective of the normative system of which it is a part. For instance, the normative reason to get a medical check-up is that prudence requires it. Motivating reasons, by contrast, justify actions only from the perspective of that very reason. It's difficult to understand what this claim could mean, though. If Terry eats an apple, and this is motivated by Terry's wanting to eat an apple, how does this show that Terry's action is justified, even from this perspective of his want? Perhaps we could make sense of this suggestion if we also hold that the desire to V involves thinking that V-ing would be good in some way or other. For then we could see how the motivating reason provides a perspective from which the action it motivates can be seen as justified.

Fortunately, Smith makes a second attempt to account for why both motivating reasons and normative reasons are indeed reasons. In his book *The Moral Problem*, (Smith, 1994) explains that both motivating reasons and normative reasons make actions *intelligible*. We can *understand* why an agent acts as she does by citing the reasons of either sort. But motivating reasons and normative reasons render actions intelligible in different ways: normative reasons, by showing what's really to be said for the action; motivating reasons, by showing us how the action came about. And this is the only common feature possessed by the two.

Is this correct? And is this enough? There's little doubt that reasons render actions intelligible. But things other than reasons render actions intelligible too. The sunlight renders many actions intelligible: when it's pitch black, you can't determine very well what other people are doing. The sunlight thus helps you to understand many actions. But the fact that sunlight renders actions intelligible does not suffice to make sunlight a reason for anything. So we shouldn't be too quick to conclude that both psychological attitudes and normative facts are reasons, just because they too can make actions intelligible. More seems to be needed.

Fortunately, Smith articulates a particular *way* to understand the relation between motivating reasons and normative reasons, a way that aims to justify classifying both psychological attitudes and normative facts as reasons. How are these two connected?

Start with the simple idea that to think that something is good or desirable is just to desire it: thinking that it is good to climb Mt. Everest is just to desire to climb it. This can't be quite right, though, because there are many things that we believe to be good (e.g. exercising) that we nonetheless fail to desire. So it's better to say: to think that something is good is just to desire it *if one is rational*. If this is correct, then if you believe that a rational person would in fact desire to V, you also ought to believe it is good or desirable to V. Your evaluative beliefs are to track your beliefs about what a rational person would want to do.

Or roughly so. For we should not just assume from the start that all rational people want the same things. And we want to bear in mind the Ownership Constraint, the thought that rationality is appropriately related to one's identity. So Smith focuses attention upon not just what any old rational person would want. He asks you to think about what a rational version of *yourself* would want. That is, imagine a person who is completely rational but otherwise exactly like you, your rational doppelgänger. Your *normative reasons*, Smith proposes, are related to your perfectly rational double's *motivating reasons*.

There is something appealing about the thought that you have normative reason to do just what you would want to do were you ideally rational. For if you were indeed rational, there would be no gap between your wants and your reasons. Your reasons would then be in a position to *explain* what you would do, thereby seeming to satisfy the Explanatory Constraint. Since the wants in question are still in some sense *your* wants, this way to understand reasons also apparently satisfies the Ownership Constraint. And since the wants in questions are those you would have if you were ideally *rational*, this account seems to satisfy the Normative Constraint. Smith's theory of reasons promises to have everything we should want in a theory of reasons.

Still, there remain some kinks in the proposal as so far sketched. For it is not quite right to say that you have normative reason to do what your rational doppelgänger would want to do. Most obviously, as we saw in Chapter 3, it is plausible that you have normative reason to do all sorts of particular things to *remedy* your irrationality; for example, perhaps you should take another course in logic, or to talk to a psychotherapist. It's also plausible that you have reason to do things to neutralize your irrationality: perhaps when in the grocery store it's not a good idea to walk through the ice cream aisle in order to make your way back to the milk section. But your perfectly rational doppelgänger presumably would have no need or desire to do such things, for he or she is already maximally rational, and thus not vulnerable to the kinds of woes you face. So it would be a mistake to say that you have normative reason to do only what your ideally rational doppelgänger would want to do.

In light of this worry, Smith articulates a different way that your reasons relate to your ideally rational doppelgänger's desires. While not identical, there is still a tight connection between these two sorts of things. Although your ideally rational doppelgänger does not need, say, to take a course in logic, he or she presumably would *tell you* to take such a course. That is, your perfect double would want you to act in particular ways, and *those* are the ways that you have reason to act. You don't have reason to mimic a good role model or *example*. You instead have reason to do what such a person advises you to do. This, then, is Smith's *advice model* of reasons for action. The advice model is superior to the example model, in that only the former can account for the reasons that stem from our rational imperfections.

The appeal of relating reasons to an ideally rational agent or deliberator is undeniable. For it helps us to satisfy the Normative

Constraint. But idealizing comes at a cost. The worry is that by making adjustments that capture the sense in which reasons justify the actions that they are reasons for, we lose our grip on the sense in which reasons explain the actions that they are reasons for. Williams seemed to meet the Explanatory Constraint quite easily, because for him all reasons were ultimately grounded in the agent's actual subjective motives, not the motives of some ideal agent (not even an ideal version of yourself.) It is true that Williams idealizes somewhat in correcting for some of the agent's mistaken beliefs, but for him reasons are still related to the agent's *actual* motives. Thus it is no mystery how an agent's reasons have explanatory power. But Smith's account relates reasons to what someone *else* wants: specifically, what your ideal doppelgänger would have you do.

There are two distinct problems with such a move. First, while your ideal doppelgänger might *want* you to do various things, these wants are not themselves motives, but more like wishes. They don't explain anything you do. But psychologism is appealing largely because it purports to relate reasons to psychological items that are *intrinsically* motivational. Your doppelgänger's wants are not like that. So it's not immediately clear how your doppelgänger's wishes can explain anything, or at least not in the way that reasons are thought to explain the actions for which they are reasons. So we might wonder whether the advice model can adequately meet the Explanatory Constraint.

Second, it's not immediately clear how your doppelgänger's desires are reasons for *you*, for your doppelganger's desires are not really your desires, and it's not obvious why the former necessarily generate the reasons the latter can. You might wonder why you should even care what your rational doppelgänger wants to do, or wants you to do. You don't own your rational doppelgänger's motives, and so you might feel alienated from what he or she would like for you to do. Of course, if you *do* happen to want to be ideal in the way that your ideal doppelganger is, the gap is closed and there is no problem: you will be motivated to do what you think your ideal doppelganger would want you to do. But you might not want to be ideal in that way; it seems to be a contingent matter whether you do. So it's unclear whether Smith's advice model can adequately meet the Ownership Constraint. (This is actually a potential problem for the example model as well.)

In order to see how Smith can neutralize these problems, we should understand better how Smith construes the notion of rationality, and how he thinks your own conception of what your ideally rational self is like can *genuinely* motivate *specifically* you. So just how *does* your rational doppelgänger differ from you? Are the differences minor enough to dodge the threat of alienation?

Smith's understanding of *rational deliberation* is more ambitious than that of Williams and other Davidsonians. Smith does agree that your reasons aren't simply a function of your actual desires, because you might be mistaken about "the facts." So, as with Williams, when thinking about how you could deliberate rationally from your current desires, we may correct for your faulty beliefs about the facts. For genuinely rational deliberation is from the standpoint of one is who well informed. Smith also acknowledges that rational deliberation includes things like the pursuit of the means to your ends, the specification of ways to accomplish your general goals, and most of the other uncontroversial deliberative processes Williams already identifies. (By contrast, Smith is skeptical about the extent to which the exercise of the imagination is genuinely rational.) And none of these forms of deliberating seem very alienating: discovering that you would be motivated to V if you were better informed is itself a good way to be motivated to V.

But Smith holds that most people who successfully engage in these forms of garden-variety deliberation can still fall short of full rationality. For Smith specifies a way of rationally deliberating that goes beyond the usual list. He explains that you can consider whether your various desires (and other pro-attitudes and subjective motives) are *systematically* justifiable. The desires of fully rational people are not ad hoc; they mesh together in mutually supportive ways. You can determine whether the various objects of your desires are things that fit together well. And if by desiring something new or by ceasing to desire something unsupported, you can make the entire set of your desires more *unified*, then you are to that extent more rational. Realizing this can lead you to actually acquire unifying desires, and to discard unsupported desires, thereby exercising your rational powers.

Smith offers little in the way of example to illustrate how such a form of rational deliberation might go. So, we must be inventive. Imagine you have a standing desire to eat tom yum. Imagine you also have a standing desire to eat panang curry. Finally, suppose you have a standing desire to eat pla goong. This set of desires would be more unified were a more general desire to eat Thai food added to it. For this more general desire to eat Thai food would, to some extent, explain and justify the three more specific desires you already have. If you find each of these three meals good, it stands to reason that, as far as these things go, you find Thai food generally good. And realizing this can cause you to desire to eat Thai food, resulting in a set of desires that is more systemically unified than the one with which you began.

So Smith supplements the received list of ways that you can deliberate rationally from your current desires or motives. You can add and discard desires on the ground that your resulting desiderative profile is more systematically justifiable. A rational deliberator is thus not only well informed, takes appropriate means, etc.—but also makes his or her desires as systematically justifiable as possible.

Relevantly, the process of systematic justification seems unlikely to generate significant alienation. The process is to make your set of current desires more coherent, making it more likely 1) that you get what you want, and 2) that you understand why you want what you want. None of this should estrange you.

But how transformative is this process of systematic justification? Will adding and subtracting desires in the aforementioned way really make all that much of a difference? One might think that it will clean things up around the edges, but still leave much of one's idiosyncratic motivations intact. (In fact, in order to ward off the threat of alienation, one should hope it would.) Smith, however, is extremely optimistic. He insists that everyone can deliberate to arrive at the *same set* of desires by engaging in a process of systematic justification of their given desires (1994, p 173). No matter with what desires you begin, unifying your set of desires will leave you wanting the very same things that others who undergo the same process want. Iggy Pop and Margaret Thatcher, despite their initial differences, would want the same things (relative to their differing circumstances) were each to unify their respective desiderative profiles!

Now, this philosophical argument may sound like wishful thinking. What reason is there to think that everyone who deliberates in these specific ways will really wind up being motivated to do the same things?

Smith's argument rests primarily upon his analysis of the *concept* of a normative reason. He thinks that it is simply part of our collective idea of what a reason is that what counts as a reason for one person in some set of circumstances must be the same as for any other person in the same circumstances. That is, to think of reasons as *relative* to individuals is to be confused. Normative reasons are instead non-relative. When we ask whether there is a reason to V in circumstances C, we do not need to know who the relevant agent is. It is not as though that in circumstances C agent A has a reason to V but in the very same circumstances agent B has a reason not to V. When we talk about (normative) reasons *simpliciter*, we are thinking of a normative concept that applies generally, not idiosyncratically.

To make this more plausible, Smith operates with a very broad conception as what counts as *circumstances*. The circumstances in which you decide include not only the various *external* facts that shape the desirability of your many action-options, but also *psychological* factors that affect the rationality of your resulting choices. Smith specifically highlights a person's tastes as an element of one's circumstances. For instance, if you prefer wine to beer, while I prefer beer to wine, then you and I do not face the same circumstances when each of us orders a drink at the bar. What you have reason to order depends upon all of your circumstances, including your tastes.

On the surface, this just looks like the reintroduction of psychological attitudes as the relevant grounding factor for not only motivating reasons but also normative reasons. If psychological attitudes such as tastes or preferences are tightly related to both types of reasons, what justifies distinguishing reasons into these two sorts anyway?

The answer for Smith lies in the different ways preferences generate the two different kinds of reasons. In most situations, your preference for wine will influence not only what you are motivated to order, but also what you have normative reason to order. Usually, those who like wine should order wine rather than beer. But tastes don't always so determine normative reasons. An ordinary person with a taste for, say, heroin may very well have a motivating reason to shoot up. But a preference for heroin, I venture, does not typically generate a normative reason to shoot up. For a perfectly rational person who nonetheless has a taste for

heroin will presumably not make it her goal to shoot up. Her taste
for heroin, though part of her circumstances, need not motivate her
to pursue it. And if a perfectly rational person who finds herself
in a set of circumstances in which she has a taste for heroin is not
motivated to use heroin, then anyone in those circumstances lacks
a normative reason to use heroin. So the way tastes and preferences
relate to motivating reasons differs from the way tastes and preferences relate to normative reasons.

In light of this, we now can reassess Smith's claim (or the
implication of his claim) that the ideally rational doppelgänger
of Margaret Thatcher would want to do the same things wanted
by the ideally rational doppelgänger of Iggy Pop, were they to
face identical circumstances. For their tastes are elements of their
circumstances. Much of the initial resistance to Smith's view
probably stems from awareness of the fact that Pop and Thatcher
have such different tastes. And this thought makes it difficult to
assess what they would be motivated to do were they somehow
to have the *same* tastes and preferences, and even more difficult to
assess what they would be motivated to do were they also practically rational. It may no longer seem so obvious that they would
not be identically motivated were they both to undergo such
sweeping transformations. Unlike, say, Williams, Smith is happy to
idealize away.

But remaining skepticism about Smith's claim lingers, I suspect,
from doubts about whether the process of systematically justifying
desires would really modify each person's motivations radically
enough to yield identical motivations for all. Smith may very well
be correct that our concept of a (normative) reason is non-relative,
and so perfectly rational people facing exactly the same circumstances would have the same reasons. And he may also be correct
to say that our concept of being rational is a summary notion: a
rational person is, *among other things*, 1) well-informed, 2) technically efficient, and 3), yes, systematically unified in her desires. But
if rationality is completely non-relative, then the list of qualities
that together sum up to rationality must extend beyond the specific
traits Smith (and others) mentions. The Heartless Husband may
very well be motivated to treat his wife more nicely if he were
perfectly *rational*, but it is still highly doubtful that his motivations
would much improve if he were only well informed, technically
efficient, had desires that are systematically justified, *and nothing*

further. This list of specific traits that Smith (or Williams) identifies as elements of rationality all seem compatible with highly unreasonable behavior. This seems so because these traits all have a highly formal or procedural character: systematically justifying your desires, for instance, appears to leave wide open the issue of *what* it is that you desire. It is a familiar point that two people can each have completely coherent sets of psychological attitudes, even though the content of these attitudes in no way matches each other's—a point that leads most to reject a simple coherentist theory of *truth*. Even if the concept of rationality is indeed just as non-relative as the concept of truth, as Smith insists, we still should doubt that well-informed people whose desires are systematically unified are motivated to do what they have normative reason to do. To think that they would be so motivated is wildly (and unreasonably) optimistic.

Of course, it remains open to just stipulate that rationality is *whatever* set of traits the possession of which motivates you to do what you have non-relative normative reason to do. That is, we could let the notion of a normative reason completely drive our notion of what rationality is. But such a strategy runs completely counter to the spirit of psychologism, which attempts to understand reasons in terms of psychological attitudes (like beliefs, desires, motives, etc.) and/or psychological traits (like being well informed, efficient, having a unified desiderative profile, etc.) Conceding that rationality cannot be reduced to a set of *specifiable* psychological traits amounts to abandoning psychologism altogether.

What, then, is the connection between motivating reasons and normative reasons? Smith's specific answer doesn't seem right: it seems that you can have normative reasons to do things that you wouldn't have motivating reasons to do (or advise your actual self to do) even if you were well-informed, efficient, and desideratively unified. But at least Smith thinks it is necessary to account for the connection between motivating reasons and normative reasons. Is there some better way to do this?

Building motivating reasons out of normative reasons

Is THERE A different way to sustain a connection between normative reasons and motivating reasons? Rather than starting with a view of what motivating reasons are, and then attempting to construct normative reasons from some idealized version of motivating reasons—as Smith does—we might try to work in the opposite direction. First, we account for normative reasons. Normative reasons are roughly facts with some normative significance. They typically are non-psychological. For instance, you have a normative reason to go to the Sonic Youth show: they will be playing some dissonant music. You have this reason to go the show whether you know about the show or not. You may also have this reason whether you care about listening to dissonant music or not, although perhaps normative reasons are somewhat relative to tastes too. In any case, you have very many normative reasons: some you know about; some you don't; some appeal to you; some don't.

How can motivating reasons be built out of these normative reasons? We'll consider a few different strategies. The simplest is to say that if you are motivated by one of your normative reasons, then this normative reason just *is* your motivating reason. A motivating reason, on this first view, can be just a normative reason that motivates the agent whose reason it is. Motivating reasons and normative reasons aren't different beasts after all. Rather, motivating reasons are just a subset of normative reasons, the normative reasons that motivate you.

But there are at least two grounds for doubting this proposal. First, we will want to revise the simplest view if we doubt that normative reasons can indeed ever motivate. How can the fact (or the truth or the event) that Sonic Youth will be playing dissonant music later motivate you to do anything now? Actions can't be motivated by something in the future. More importantly, it's hard to see how a *non-psychological* fact or a truth can motivate one to act. Isn't psychologism correct at least about *motivating* reasons?

This takes us to the more sophisticated version of this view. Both worries just mentioned can now be assuaged if a motivating reason is conceived of not as a specific type of normative reason (viz., a normative reason that motivates), but instead as a psychological attitude *whose content* is a normative reason. Motivating reasons are thus *about* normative reasons.

This sophisticated conception of a motivating reason can itself take at least three different forms, depending upon exactly how the normative reason fits into the content of the motivating reason. First, we might understand the normative reason to form the entire content of the psychological attitude that is the motivating reason. In the above example, wherein your normative reason for going to the concert is that Sonic Youth will be playing dissonant music later, we can say that your motivating reason for going to the club to be *your belief or judgment that Sonic Youth will be playing dissonant music later*. After all, it would be quite natural for someone to explain why you go to the club by mentioning that you believed that Sonic Youth will be playing dissonant music later. The belief whose content is identical to the normative reason is on this view the motivating reason. We will evaluate this proposal shortly.

For now, consider a second form of this second conception of a motivating reason. Here the motivating reason is a belief whose explicit content is a *value judgment* about the normative reason. If your normative reason for going to the club is that Sonic Youth will be playing dissonant music at the club, then your motivating reason on this view would be *your belief that it is good that Sonic Youth will be playing dissonant music at the club*. Or perhaps, your motivating reason is your belief that it would good for you to *hear* Sonic Youth play dissonant music at the club; there are, of course, a variety of ways to phrase the reason in question. Common to them all, however, is the identification of your motivating reason with your judgment that the item that is your normative reason is good in some way.

The third way to build motivating reasons out of normative reasons requires an even more complex thought from the agent whose reason it is. The content of the belief that is the motivating reason is explicitly about a normative reason. So on this third view, your motivating reason (in the case above) would be *your belief that the fact that Sonic Youth will be playing dissonant music is a normative reason to go to the show*. This belief explicitly about your normative reason is your motivating reason. The connection between motivating reasons and normative reasons is thus forged by making the very concept of a normative reason as part of the content of the motivating reason.

To summarize, there are three ways motivating reasons can be about normative reasons. A motivating reason might be a belief whose content is:

1 Sonic Youth will be playing dissonant music later *(a garden-variety fact)*, or

2 It is good that Sonic Youth will be playing dissonant music later *(an evaluative fact)*, or

3 The fact that Sonic Youth will be playing dissonant music is a normative reason to go to the show *(a normative fact)*

Let's examine each proposal in turn.

The distinct advantages of the first proposal are several. First, it demands the least cognitive sophistication of rational agents. Agents with motivating reasons construed in this way do not need to think that anything is good, nor that anything is a reason. This promises to put rational agency within the grasp of animals and young children unable to make complex evaluative and normative judgments. All that's needed is the ability to apprehend the garden-variety consideration which also *is* the normative reason for the same action. So, according to this first proposal, not only reflective agents have motivating reasons.

The second possibly advantageous feature of the first proposal is that it allows logical space for a sophisticated agent to act for a motivating reason that she believes is not at all good or normatively justified. Consider an unwilling email addict who is yet again motivated to check her email by her belief that there might be something new in her inbox. She can do this *even if* she doesn't believe that the fact that there might be something new in her inbox is a normative reason for her to check her email. And, it may seem, she can do this even if she doesn't believe that there's anything good about knowing whether there is something new in her inbox. She can view her own addiction for what it is: a distraction and a complete waste of time. But since she is in the grip of her belief that there might be something new in her inbox, it can motivate her to do what even she herself does not value. Reasons can motivate you to act, it may seem, even if you don't think that there is anything good or justifiable about so acting. (And, we can maintain neutrality about whether the fact that there might be something new in her inbox really *is* a normative reason for her to check her email. That is, we can grant—if we want to—that this consideration really *is* a normative reason, all the while acknowledging that the agent herself need not view it as such in order to be motivated by this consideration.)

But there are powerful reasons to reject this first proposal. For it identifies motivating reasons with beliefs in garden-variety facts. And, although this view has been multiply defended, it remains highly doubtful that a person can be motivated by such a belief alone. It's plausible that our email addict is motivated to check her email not only by believing that there might be something new in her inbox, but also by her desire to read anything that's new in her inbox. In any case, actions aren't motivated just by garden-variety beliefs alone. So motivating reasons are not simply beliefs in garden-variety facts, such as the belief that there might be something new in one's inbox. *Whatever* they are, motivating reasons seem to involve more than this.

If beliefs alone can't be motivating reasons, then it appears that this first proposal is in no worse shape than the other two proposals we're considering, each of which also identifies a motivating reason with a belief. Why think that this first proposal is in any worse shape than the second or the third, which also identify a motivating reason with a belief?

To see why, let's consider the third proposal (for instance) more explicitly. Recall that the third proposal says that your motivating reason for heading to the show is your belief that the fact that Sonic Youth will be playing dissonant music is a normative reason to go to the show. This belief is not a belief in some garden-variety fact; it is instead a belief that some garden-variety fact is itself a normative reason. Now, it seems plausible that you would believe that this garden-variety fact is a normative reason for you to go the show only if you are motivated to go. It's perhaps because you want to hear some dissonant music that you are disposed to believe that the fact that Sonic Youth will be playing dissonant music is a normative reason for you to go to the show. If you were indifferent to hearing dissonant music, then you wouldn't think that the fact that Sonic Youth will be playing dissonant music is any reason for you to head to the show. So, on this proposal, a motivating reason is not a desire, but it is the kind of belief that an agent has only if she also has the right kind of desire.

This is why the third proposal does not succumb to the same objection that applies to the first proposal. By identifying a motivating reason with a belief in a garden-variety fact, the first proposal is vulnerable to the charge that it portrays agents as somehow motivated to do things that they have no desire (or pro-attitude) to do. For there's nothing odd or irrational about believing that Sonic Youth will be playing dissonant music at the concert, and being utterly unmoved by this belief. Believing *this* obviously does not require being motivated to do *anything* in particular. But believing that the fact that Sonic Youth will play dissonant music is a normative reason for you to go—believing *that*—plausibly does require that you want something in particular, namely, to witness some mind-bending cacophony. So although the third proposal identifies a motivating reason with a belief, it does not presume that one can be motivated by such a reason in the absence of a pro-attitude or a desire. On the contrary, there is good reason to think that having a relevant pro-attitude or desire is necessary for having this peculiar sort of belief.

The second proposal, which identifies a motivating reason with a belief about the *goodness* of something, aims to capture the strengths of the first and third proposals while avoiding their flaws. Remember that one advantage of the first proposal is that it allows us to understand how cognitively unsophisticated agents can be rationally motivated—it required them only to have the wherewithal to have beliefs about garden-variety facts; it does not require them to have any comparatively grandiose beliefs about normative reasons. The second proposal lies between these two. It doesn't demand that all rational agents have any beliefs about normative reasons, but it does require them to be capable of thinking that something is good. It says that agents are motivated by the thought that, e.g. hearing some dissonant music by heading over to the Sonic Youth show would be good in some way. This is not the crudest of thoughts, to be sure. But, as just about any parent of a typical toddler knows, it doesn't take all the much brainpower to think that something is good (or, even more clearly, bad). Evaluative thoughts such as these seem less intellectually demanding than the corresponding thoughts about normative reasons. So this second proposal is, in this one respect, more plausible than the third (though perhaps not as plausible as the first).

But there is also at least one way the second proposal seems better than the first. Much like the third proposal, the second proposal identifies a motivating reason with a belief that plausibly motivates only those who also already have a corresponding pro-attitude or desire. That is, if the thought that it would be in some way good for you to go to the Sonic Youth show motivates you to head there, then you must also want something that you would get by so going. It's arguable that there is a tight link between evaluative belief and desire: those who believe it would be good to V also have some sort of desire or pro-attitude or subjective motive toward V-ing. Note that Williams (1981) *defined* the term "subjective motive" to characterize, among other things, evaluative belief. So it's not crazy to think that those with evaluative beliefs have the pro-attitudes necessary for them to be motivated to do what they believe is good. This second proposal does not have the same weakness had by the first.

One of the advantages of the first proposal was that it made logical room for an agent to act for a reason that she believes is not at all good or normatively justified. Akrasia, on the first proposal, is clearly possible. But the second proposal does *almost* as well as the first on this score. On this view, agents motivated by a reason to act see their action as good in *some* way or other. But this is surely compatible with thinking that they are not justified in so acting. And even the third proposal is fairly plausible as well: while it insists that an agent who acts intentionally thinks she has some normative reason in so acting, she need not think that she has best or most reason to act that way. So there is room for her to think that she shouldn't be acting act as she is.

To summarize the advantages of these three proposals, each of which identified a motivating reason with a belief:

I Motivating reason = garden-variety belief

Advantages:

- Makes room for brutish rational agents,
- Makes room for akrasia.

Disadvantages:

- Garden-variety beliefs alone don't motivate.

II *Motivating reason = evaluative belief*

Advantages:

- Makes room for toddlers as rational agents.

- Makes room for akrasia.

- Evaluative beliefs, either by themselves or with what they presuppose, motivate.

III *Motivating reason = belief that one has a normative reason*

Advantages:

- These beliefs, either by themselves or with what they presuppose, motivate.

Disadvantages:

- There is room for only adult-like human beings to be motivated by reasons.

- Might not make enough room for akrasia.

The second interpretation of motivating reasons, which understands them to be evaluative beliefs, seems to the best of the three. On this view, if your normative reason for going to the show is that Sonic Youth will be playing dissonant music there, your motivating reason is (or could be) that you believe that it is in some way good or desirable that Sonic Youth will be playing dissonant music there. Your motivating reason can explain what motivates you to go to the show. Moreover, your normative reason counts in favor of going to the show. This seems to me to be the most plausible version of the hybrid view, but it is certainly possible to favor either of the other interpretations of motivating reasons.

I want to conclude this section by noting one more problem with the first and second versions of the sophisticated strategy of building motivating reasons out of normative reasons. Only the third version of the strategy *really* builds motivating reasons out of normative reasons. That is, the first two build motivating reasons on the idea that normative reasons *can* serve as the content of the psychological attitudes that are the motivating reasons. If the fact that Sonic Youth will be playing dissonant music is a normative reason for you to go to the club, then your belief that (it is good that) Sonic Youth will be playing dissonant music can be your motivating reason for going. But you might also have this motivating reason even if the fact that Sonic Youth will be playing dissonant music *isn't* a normative reason for going. It seems you can be motivated by reasons that just aren't normative reasons. If so, then the first and second versions have not shown how motivating reasons are built out of normative reasons. And this seems to be a problem.

So, in the end, I'm not sure which version of this strategy is the best of the three. But next let us consider an important challenge to the very idea that motivating reasons and normative reasons are at all distinct.

The identity thesis

IF THE HYBRID view is right, then we can meet the Explanatory Constraint by showing how motivating reasons explain the actions for which they are reasons, while meeting the Normative Constraint by showing how normative reasons justify the actions for which they are reasons. And that would be fabulous. But this way of solving the problem may feel vaguely unsatisfying. Multiplying the types of reasons that there are in order to meet the various Constraints simultaneously can seem like, well, cheating. It's hard to think of a philosophical debate about some *other* fundamental concept where going hybrid is widely viewed to be an acceptable move.

Dissatisfaction with hybridity is expressed by a sizable and prestigious minority of those who work on reasons, by philosophers who see reasons for action as bound up with *both* the explanation and the justification of action at once:

> The concept of a reason for action stands at the point of intersection, so to speak, between the theory of the explanation of actions and the theory of their justification. (Woods, 1972, p 189)

If something can be a reason for action, then it could be someone's reason for acting on a particular occasion, and it would then figure in an explanation of that action. (Williams, 1981, p 6)

The reason why you ought to do an action and the reason why you do it can be the same. (Korsgaard, 1986, p 10)

A reason must be something for which someone could have acted, and in any case where someone does act for that reason, the reason contributes to the explanation of her action. (Dancy, 1995, p 4)

By the [identity thesis], I mean that when an agent acts for a (specific) reason that very reason is also the explanation (or at least part of the explanation) of why she did what she did. Normative or justificatory reasons and explanatory reasons are the same reasons in such a case, and not different kinds of reasons altogether ... [The identity thesis] can be interpreted as expressing nothing more than the everyday assumption that we sometimes act for reasons, that is: that we do something because it is right or justified. (Heuer, 2004, pp 45, 47)

I don't mean to pretend that they aren't important differences among the views of these various thinkers. There are. But they all agree that there is not a sharp divide between the reasons that motivate, and the reasons that justify. Ulrike Heuer calls this view *the identity thesis*, and she defines it in opposition to what I've been calling the hybrid view. The identity thesis is essentially the thesis that there is only one kind of reason for action. (There still might be separate reasons *why* an event, such as an action, takes place, as we saw in Chapter 1.) One and the same reason can potentially both explain and justify the action for which it is reason. The identity thesis seems most compelling when thinking about reasons from the first-person perspective: the reason that counts in favor of your V-ing can be the very reason you do indeed V. That is, you can V for the very reason that makes V-ing the thing to do (Garrard and McNaughton, 1998; Norman, 2001).

This is not to say that *all* reasons for action in fact both explain and justify actions. That would be absurd. A reason can justify without explaining, simply because you don't do what that reason supports. For example, spending a week in Hawaii would be pleasant, and is a reason for you to buy a ticket to Hawaii, even if this reason does not explain any action of yours, because you never buy a ticket to go there. All the same, the reason for you to buy a ticket is potentially explanatory, because you in some sense could buy a ticket to Hawaii for this reason. This reason *can* both explain and justify one and the same action, and so it really is a reason *for* that action.

More controversially, not all reasons for action that motivate action actually count in favor of the actions they motivate. For example, that furtively killing your landlord would feel gratifying might be the reason for which you kill him, but that it would feel gratifying does not justify or even count in favor of killing him. We are inclined to say instead that this is a very bad reason for killing him. But that it would feel gratifying is indeed *a* reason for killing him, only because that it would feel gratifying *often* or *usually* counts in favor of doing things that feel gratifying. (Contrast this to the consideration that it would feel frustrating, which typically does not count in favor of doing things that feel frustrating.) That it would feel gratifying is both the *sort* of thing that can motivate action and is the *sort* of thing that can justify or count in favor of action. And this remains so even in the odd circumstance where the reason does not count in favor of the action for which it is a reason. Defenders of the identity thesis thus typically hold that while motivation and justification can come apart in specific cases, in the standard cases they travel together.

So much for explaining what the identity thesis *is*. Why think that the identity thesis is *true*? Proponents of the identity thesis tend to rely on the intuitive plausibility of slogans like those contained in the quotes above. It appears to be conceptually true that we can act for the reasons that count in favor of so acting. *If* one reason in favor of playing Scrabble is that playing Scrabble is fun, I should be able to play Scrabble for that very reason. It would be very odd if I could not play Scrabble for the reason that in fact counts in favor of playing Scrabble, but only for a different reason, such as that I believe that it would be fun to play Scrabble. To be sure, when I play Scrabble for the reason that playing Scrabble is fun, I do indeed believe that it would be fun to play Scrabble. But *that belief* is not itself my reason for playing Scrabble. My reason for playing Scrabble, it seems, is (or, at least, can be) the reason that counts in favor of playing Scrabble.

Though intuitively plausible, the Identity Thesis is not obviously true. But it's hard to know what to say in response to those who deny it. It seems to me that the burden of proof lies squarely upon those who reject the Identity Thesis. We should have a very good reason for thinking that the reasons for which we act always differ from the reasons that count in favor of our actions. Perhaps rejecting the Identity Thesis will turn out to be the only way to meet all the other desiderata of a philosophical account of reasons, in which case we probably should not worry too much about the fact that our best account of reasons is a hybrid theory. But other things being equal, it seems preferable to have an account of reasons that meets all of the Constraints we have identified *as well as* complies with the Identity Thesis. That would be ideal.

Nevertheless, in the next chapter I'll discuss a reason for thinking that the hybrid theory is false, a reason apart from the Identity Thesis. But it doesn't take out just the hybrid theory. It's actually a reason for thinking that *all* of the accounts of reasons we've discussed so far—psychologism, factualism, non-factive views, hybrid views—are false, or at best radically incomplete.

CHAPTER SIX

Constitutivism

Here we have been focusing upon reasons for *action*. The hope of adopting this strategy was that we would learn something about the nature of reasons by restricting our attention to one particular kind of reason. In this chapter, I introduce a different way to think about reasons, one that takes this restriction of focus very seriously. We might call this way *constitutivism*.

Constitutivists hold that understanding what reasons for action requires first (or simultaneously) understanding what action is. It is hopeless, they think, to assume that actions are primitive or simple or exogenous, and then hunt around for what reasons for action might be. Instead, the strategy constitutivists advocate is to unlock the nature of action, and then at least the framework for thinking about reasons for action will come into view. An account of action and an account of reasons for action must be developed together.

So, then, what *is* action? More specifically, are there any features of action that might determine the kinds of considerations that serve as reasons for action? First, we'll briefly investigate the claim that action necessarily aims at the pleasure of the agent, a view that is called *psychological hedonism*. If true, this could serve as a key premise in an argument establishing *rational hedonism*, the view that one has reason to act in ways that please oneself.

Second, we will look at several related claims that understand action and agency as linked closely to autonomy, self-knowledge, or one's self-conception. If accurate, this could serve as a key premise in an argument establishing that reasons for action relate to knowing and/or ruling oneself.

Activities and aims

CONSTITUTIVISTS ALL HOLD that we need to understand the nature of action if we are to make sense of the notion of a reason for action. Action is often distinguished from other behaviors and processes by noting that action has a constitutive aim, an aim without which the action wouldn't even be a full-fledged action. Action is what it is in part because of what it aims at. This thought might be fruitful, because if action has a constitutive aim, then perhaps it can be argued that reasons for action are related to the standard(s) of correctness implied by this constitutive aim.

Let's take some time to unpack this complex thought. Action isn't the only thing with a constitutive aim. Playing soccer, for instance, has a constitutive aim. If you are playing soccer, you aim to help your team score more goals than the opposing team. And the rules of soccer shape how you can do this. If, indifferent to the rules of soccer, you pick up the ball and run toward your opponent's goal, then you just aren't playing soccer at all. And if you don't care whether your team or the other team scores goals, you aren't playing soccer either. Setting draws aside, to play soccer is to aim to score more goals than the other team, all by (or at least while) following the rules of soccer.

This aim provides us with a standard for evaluating whether someone is playing soccer well or poorly. If a soccer player is running very slowly, then this usually does not help his team score more goals than the opposing team—indeed, it helps the other team score more goals. So his running slowly can be criticized by the very standards constitutive of the activity he himself is performing: he is performing poorly by the standards of soccer. Whether he *wants* to run slowly or quickly is largely irrelevant, because the game of soccer he is playing is itself the source of the standards for evaluating his running. In this way, an activity can provide constitutive standards for evaluating the performances of those engaged in the activity.

Now it is obvious that playing soccer is an optional activity. While our slow running soccer player's performance is a bit of bad soccer-playing, no matter what *he* thinks about it, he is under no obligation to play soccer. If he stops playing soccer, the practice of soccer no longer governs him. His slow running would then not be a bit of bad soccer-playing. The norms of soccer are escapable.

With this example in mind, we now may ask a couple questions. Is action or agency itself at all like soccer, in that it has some constitutive aims that provide standards for evaluating actions? And if so, is action or agency *un*like soccer, in that these standards for evaluating actions are *in*escapable?

The idea that action has an inescapable constitutive aim is most often illustrated by discussing parallel ideas about the nature of belief. What is it, after all, to believe something? Here's a common enough thought: to believe p is to take p to be *true*.[1] There seems to be some internal connection between belief and truth. We want to say that belief aims at the truth. And its aiming at the truth is not optional: it's not as though someone can sincerely believe things without their beliefs at least aiming to be sensitive to evidence for and against the truth of what they believe. Although someone can *say* "I don't care if what I believe is true," systemic indifference to evidence of truth threatens to render the description of such a person's attitudes as beliefs unintelligible. If your beliefs really aren't responsive to considerations relevant to evidence for the truth of what you believe, that it's hard to see why it's appropriate to characterize your attitudes really as *beliefs* in the first place, rather than as hopes, wishes, or something else altogether.

One very nice feature of this fact about belief is that it provides us with an internal justification for believing the truth. David Velleman puts this point like this:

Belief aims at the truth in the normative sense only because it aims at the truth descriptively, in the sense that it is constitutively regulated by mechanisms designed to ensure that it is true. (2000, p 17)

We can extract a norm about how we *should* believe based upon what it *is* to believe. More specifically, the nature of belief tells us something about reasons for belief. So the person who questions whether she has a reason to believe what's true isn't really asking a legitimate question. The justification for believing the truth doesn't come from something external to the nature of belief itself. So, believing the truth isn't justified (merely) on the grounds that doing so will get you what you want, or that it will make you happy, or contribute to your reproductive success. Rather, if you are even in the business of believing things, you thereby have reason to believe what's true. Truth is the constitutive aim of belief, and so reasons to believe are necessarily related to considerations concerning the truth of what's believed.

But believing things, unlike soccer, appears to be inescapable. We just *do* believe things; *pace* the Skeptics, we can't completely suspend belief in everything. So it was misleading a moment ago for me to write "if you are even in the business of believing things ..." For we are in that business. And much like Michael Corleone, we can't leave it.

Now, this brief sketch of the constitutive aim of belief, and of how this aim generates reasons for belief, can surely be questioned. I don't assume that it is true. But it is very plausible, and, more importantly, it provides us with a model for thinking about how action too might have a constitutive aim, and, if so, how this aim might likewise generate reasons for action. And understanding reasons for action is our quarry here.

So thinking about things this way forces us to ask: what *is* it to act? When we act, is there some target at which we aim in so acting, in much the way we aim to believe the truth? Does this aim at least partially constitute what it is to act? And does this aim thereby supply us with a standard of correctness for action? Is acting inescapable? And does this standard help us understand what a *reason* for action is?

Hedonism

LET'S TACKLE THESE admittedly vague and abstract questions by first examining hedonism. I don't mean to imply that hedonism is very plausible; in fact, I think it's pretty clearly wrong. But hedonism is a fairly popular view, especially among moderately well-educated non-philosophers. And hedonism is a view that can seem easy to understand. So, by supposing that the constitutive aim of action is pleasure, we can learn something about how *any* constitutivist theory could work.

It is common to hear the claim that when people act, they necessarily act so as to attain pleasure for themselves. That is, whatever it is people do, they do it only if they believe that they will thereby by pleased. Epicurus (Inwood and Gerson, 1994), for one, wrote that "we recognized [pleasure] as our first innate good, and this is our starting point for every choice and avoidance, and we come to this by judging every good by the criterion of feeling." (Letter to Menoeceus, Diogenes Laertius, 10.129) This view—that pleasure is the goal of every action—is known as *psychological hedonism*.

Now it's one thing to say that pleasure is the goal of every action. It's another to say that action is what it is *because* it aims at pleasure—to say that a process or a bit of behavior counts as an action in virtue of the fact that it aims at pleasure. It's possible to agree with Epicurus that pleasure is, as a matter of fact, the starting point for every choice, while denying that we must choose pleasure for it to count as a choice. But let's not worry too much about this difference. Let's suppose that every action aims at pleasure only if pleasure is indeed the *constitutive* aim of action.

Even so, whatever the actual merits of psychological hedonism, we can see how its truth would be relevant for evaluating the plausibility of *rational hedonism*, the view that one has reason to V just in case V-ing would be pleasant to do. For if aiming at pleasure is indeed a constitutive aim of acting, then it makes sense to think that rational action will, at a minimum, accomplish that aim. Let's quickly acknowledge that the truth of psychological hedonism would not all by itself *guarantee* the truth of rational hedonism. For it's not exactly illogical to think both that 1) all action necessarily aims at pleasure, and 2) the fact than Agnes would be pleased to V is no reason for her to V. But if you wanted to defend rational hedonism, you'd find it much easier to do so if you had already established that action is what it is in virtue of its aiming at pleasure. If people necessarily act for the sake of pleasure, then it seems like action is successful and correct at least in so far as it accomplishes this aim. And if pleasant action is correct action, then reasons for an action would seem to be considerations that show that the act in question is or would indeed be pleasant.

Note how the constitutive aim strategy manages to capture nicely both the explanatory and the normative dimension of practical reasons. Suppose you go to the movies, and that your ultimate aim here (as with every action) is pleasure. What motivates you to go? Pleasure. Pleasure, and the considerations that suggest that going to the movies would indeed be pleasant. What's good about going to the movies? Again, pleasure—*if* it's true that going to the movies would be pleasant. So the item that motivates you is also that which makes, or would make, your action good. The constitutive aim of action can both explain and justify the actions aiming at it.

If action itself supplies us with everything we need to understand reasons for action, this is exciting. For then we can meet most or all of the various requirements that we have identified as desirable for a theory of reasons. We can show how reasons can motivate action. We can show how reasons can justify action. Finally, we can show how reasons are owned by the agent whose reasons they are, since your reasons are an aim of *yours*, rather than something externally imposed upon you.

So if pleasure were the constitutive aim of action, perhaps we could rest content. But is psychological hedonism really true? Psychological hedonism can seem tempting, for it purports to explain the real motives lying behind the stories we tell ourselves. And no doubt much apparently unselfish or altruistic behavior is in fact rooted in some kind of self-interest. Often we help others for reasons that have more to do with ourselves than with our supposed beneficiaries. But there are several reasons for doubting that the pleasure of the agent is always the constitutive aim of action. Sometimes we do things for reasons wholly other than pleasure, such as compassion, revenge, and pride. It's painfully clear that so much of what we do aims at things other than pleasure. In fact, much action aims at considerations known to be on the whole positively unpleasant. Still, we might now be spurred to look for other more plausible accounts of action's constitutive aim. Action may not always aim at pleasure, but is there something else at which it always aims?

There are various Kantian accounts of the nature of action that hope to sustain a different sort of connection between action and reasons. Kant himself held that there was an *a priori* connection between full-blooded action, autonomous action, and morally worthy action. When we (truly) act, we act autonomously, not determined by anything other than our will. And when we act autonomously, we act from a sense of duty, and so our actions have moral worth. Thus action in the fullest sense of the word is action that is good. The nature of action supplies us with the criterion for discriminating rational action from its pretenders.

But it's safe to say that the Kantian account of moral and rational action, in its pure and original form, has persuaded few, alas.[2] Even so, many have hoped to develop and defend some sort of attenuated Kantianism. Let's consider some of these efforts.

Action and knowledge

WHAT'S DISTINCTIVE ABOUT action? Various philosophers have emphasized the fact that full-blooded intentional action differs from mere behavior in that an agent *knows* what she is intentionally doing in a distinctive way (Velleman, 2000; Setiya, 2007; Anscombe, 2000). Intentional actions appear to be known by the agent in a way unlike the way one knows about the other things that one "does." When you do something intentionally, you *immediately* know what you are doing. You don't have to *observe* yourself acting in a particular way: you don't know that you are reading a book about philosophy by looking at yourself, nor by inferring this from other things you know, not in the way that you know that you are, say, heating up the room.[3] It is exceedingly difficult to specify exactly what this difference amounts to, but to most it has seemed that there is *some* very important difference here that we should track. I'll characterize this difference here simply by speaking of our knowledge of our own intentional actions as *immediate*, since it doesn't seem to be mediated by our knowledge of other things.

Again, suppose you want to hear some dissonant music, and suppose you also think that if you go to the Sonic Youth show later, you will indeed hear some dissonant music. By citing these attitudes, Davidsonians can thus seem to account for why you wind up going to the show. But your psychological attitudes don't get you to go the show without *you* knowing it, at least not when you are going there for a reason. The motivation here does not operate behind your back. Rather, when you are heading to the Sonic Youth show intentionally, you know this straight away.

In fact, you know more than this. Not only do you know that you are on your way to the Sonic Youth show, but you also know that you want to hear dissonant music, and that you believe that Sonic Youth will be playing dissonant music. That is, the psychological attitudes that Davidsonians identify as reasons are psychological attitudes that you know that you have if and when they motivate you to act for this reason. You aren't unaware of the reasons for which you act. You know not only your actions, but also the psychological attitudes that supposedly are or are related to your reasons for actions.

In fact, you know even more than this. It's not as though you know what you are doing, and you know what you think and want, but you are unaware of any relation between the two. If you are heading to the Sonic Youth show because you want to hear some dissonant music and you think that Sonic Youth will be creating some dissonant music, then you typically know that you are heading there *for that reason*. You know the connection between your action and your reason. You aren't in the dark about the rational causality that operates through you and in you. You are on top of it.

In fact, even this understates the nature of your knowledge of your reasons. Suppose your psychoanalyst were to inform you that you go to Sonic Youth concerts in order to drown out the nagging voices of your parents that you've internalized. He says that you feel good at noisy concerts because only then are you distracted from the voices in your head. And suppose that you, fully respecting her expertise, accept her explanation. And suppose further that her explanation is correct. Then, you would know why you are going to Sonic Youth concerts. You would know that you go because you want to drown out the voices in your head, which you think, at some level, you can do by going to Sonic Youth concerts. In this case, your knowledge of why you do what you do is based upon the evidence of your psychoanalyst's testimony. In other words, your knowledge would be *mediated by* this evidence. You don't know *immediately* why you go to the concerts. Instead, you find out by means of knowing something *else*.

But this sort of knowledge is not like the knowledge you ordinarily have of your reasons for actions. When you act *for* a reason, you typically know non-inferentially the reason for which you are acting. If someone were to ask you for what reason you are reading this book, you would know the answer without checking up on any evidence, as another person would have to. Not only do you typically know *what* you are doing without having to watch or listen to yourself. You also know the *reason* for which you act without having to watch or listen to yourself. You know this—all of this—immediately.

In fact, even *this* understates the kind of knowledge of your intentional actions that you have. To see why, imagine a creature that knows straightaway the reason why it moves as it does, in much the way that you know straightaway whether and where you are hurting. Just as you do not suffer stomach pains without immediately knowing it, not inferring it from anything else, this creature immediately knows what and why it does what it does. This type of knowledge, though immediate, is nevertheless not *spontaneous*. It doesn't move as it does *because* it knows how it moves, just as you aren't in pain *because* you know you are in pain. To put it in Kantian terms, it doesn't operate according to its *conception* of laws. It just happens to know its movements and their causes immediately. Like other instances of "theoretical knowledge," the thing known (the pain; the movement) exists prior to the knowledge of it.

You and I, by contrast, *do* operate according to our conception of laws, at least in so far as we are acting intentionally. You intentionally do one thing in doing another *because* you know that's what you are doing. If you are going to a concert in order to spend time with your friend, then you are doing this *intentionally* because you know that's what you are up to. If you don't know what you are doing, then you aren't intentionally going to the concert to spend time with your friend; at best some unconscious drive explains why you are unintentionally going to the concert. (This is compatible with going there for that reason, and then *forgetting* your reason. It's also compatible with going to the concert out of habit, where the habit was formed because one often went to concerts to be with friends. This habit alone would not, however, make it true that spending time with a friend is *now* the reason for which you are going to the concert *this* time. Teleology is thus not sufficient for intentionality.) Practical knowledge is thus *spontaneous*, because it creates the thing it knows. This type of knowledge is indeed unlike knowledge of one's pains!

It's a strange form of knowledge, though. Usually some fact exists prior to our knowing it, a fact that remains exactly what it is whether or not anyone is aware of it. The earth was revolving around the sun before anyone knew that, and our knowing it doesn't change a thing about the earth's movements. If there is any mismatch between our believing it and the fact itself, the error lies with the belief, not with the fact.

But knowledge of one's own intentional actions is not like that. Practical knowledge is not passive; it is active. In Aquinas's parlance, it is "the cause of what it understands." There is a sense in which you know what you are doing because you are doing it, *and* a sense in which you are doing it because you know what you are doing. Further, if there is a mismatch between the intention and the action, the error lies with the action not the intention (Anscombe, 2000, p 56). To see this, consider the case where you intend to unplug the vacuum cleaner and you instead unplug the digital alarm clock. You at first don't know that you are unplugging the digital alarm clock, and the error of the mismatch lies in your action, not in your intention. You acted in error, rather than intended in error. So practical knowledge is indeed unlike knowledge of one's pains.

I admit this, though highly interesting, is rather vague. It is exceedingly difficult to characterize *exactly* how acting for a reason is connected to this idea of spontaneous knowledge. We won't be able to fully specify that here. What's important is merely to see that there is *something* interesting and unusual about the connection between practical knowledge and its object—something different about this form of knowledge from other forms—and look to see if an account of reasons for action can shed any light on this connection. Here I will just continue to call this feature of practical knowledge *spontaneity*, leaving for another day the task of accounting for the nature of *it*.

Let's summarize the ground we have covered. When you act for a reason, you typically 1) know what you are doing, 2) know your reason, 3) know that you are doing this *for* this reason. Further this knowledge is 4) immediate and 5) spontaneous. (A caveat: it might be possible to act for a reason even if one of the five conditions doesn't hold. But *when* one of these conditions fails to hold, there's something amiss about your action; your action isn't a paradigmatic instance of full-blooded intentional action.)

While our focus here is on reasons for *action*, we can easily see that knowledge of reasons for other sorts of thing is similar. Consider beliefs. When you believe p for a reason, you typically are directly aware that you believe p. You don't need someone to tell you that you believe p, nor do you need to investigate whether you believe p. If you aren't directly aware that you believe p, then you probably aren't believing p *for* a reason at all. Furthermore, not only do you typically directly know that you believe p for a reason, you also typically directly know the reason for which you believe p. That is, if you believe p for the reason that q, you typically directly know both that you believe q, and that you believe p. (Of course, there are some causes *of* your belief that you don't know about.) The reason *for* your belief is typically just as knowable as the belief itself. Not only that, but you are equally directly aware of your reason for belief *as a reason*. It's not just that if q is your reason for believing p, you are directly aware that you believe q. It's also typically true that you are aware that q is indeed your reason for believing p. That q is your reason for believing p is not something that happens behind your back. On the contrary, when you believe p for the reason that q, you are directly aware that you believe p, q, and that q is your reason for believing p. You typically are aware of the rational causality of the whole ensemble.[4]

I say "typically" because you don't *always* know all of these things. Although the way you know what you are doing is distinctive and worth understanding, it is not infallible. You can be wrong about what you're doing or believing, and you can be wrong about for what reasons you are doing or believing it. But those who rightly question the *reliability* of our "introspective" knowledge of our reasons for action or belief do not thereby discredit the claim that we typically just do immediately know our reasons. Compare: visual perception is a distinct mode of knowledge, even though it is far from perfect. We suffer from perceptual illusions, but this is compatible with perception being a distinct mode of knowledge. Likewise, the way you know your reasons is distinct, even if it too is not perfect.

Furthermore, although you typically know your reasons immediately and spontaneously, it is still possible for you also to know them in other ways. That is, if it's possible for *others* to know your reasons through observation and inference, then it is also surely possible for you to know your reasons these ways too. But the fact that it is possible for you to know your reasons through observation and inference does not entail that you cannot also know your reasons in a distinctively first-personal way. Multiple modes of knowledge are compossible.

The relation between first-personal knowledge and reasons for *emotion* is more complex. Suppose you are angry with your boss. Further, suppose this anger is not *completely* irrational; you are angry with her for a reason (*at least* one). Normally, you don't have to hunt down what this reason is. You don't have to observe yourself, or replay your memories, or ask your co-workers. You usually don't need a psychoanalyst, a personality test, a mirror, or any other evidence. You know straightaway the reason for which you are angry with her: you know your reasons for your anger just as immediately as you know *that* you are angry.

But we don't need Freud's theories to see that people often *are* unaware of their emotions, as we might in order to grasp that people have unconscious drives and beliefs. It's part of our common stock of wisdom that people are often unclear about how they feel, and about why they feel as they do. Awareness of one's own emotions is not the default; instead, often it is a significant achievement. It's a sign of great maturity to be aware of one's emotional life, rather than something guaranteed by the nature of the phenomena. Most of us are not fully aware of what we fear or wish for, whom we envy or need, and so on. So it is harder to defend an analogous thesis about the connection between knowledge and reasons for emotions: it is far from clear that typically you straightaway know your reasons for, e.g., being worried about your colleagues' opinion of you. Perhaps the heart has its reasons that Reason knows nothing about.

Even so, there may still be some connection between first-person knowledge of your emotions and the *rationality* of emotions. First off, it is nigh impossible to rationally respond to an emotion (e.g. fear of intimacy) unless you know firsthand that you have that emotion. This is most obvious in the case of total ignorance. But even if you know that you are afraid of intimacy by means of evidence—say, because your analyst tells you—and if this doesn't make your fear bubble up to consciousness, then, while your fear is indeed some sense still *yours*, you must deal with it as though it were an externally placed obstacle. Reasoning to the conclusion that intimacy is not fearful need not make this unconscious fear recede.

Second, and more importantly, semi-awareness of one's emotions is often constituted by semi-articulateness about one's own emotions. You might think to yourself: "I feel uncomfortable around my sister-in-law, but I don't know why." Only with greater self-knowledge will you be able to articulate why: e.g. "I worry that my sister-in-law will convince my brother to move away from me and my aging parents, leaving the burden of eldercare entirely upon me." Understanding why you feel the way you feel is often not much different from understanding in more detail how you feel. Grasping your reason for your emotion is grasping better the emotion itself. (Later we will see that something is similarly true about action.)

Third, unawareness of your own emotions is often viewed as itself irrational. If you yourself don't know how you feel—and this is not simply because there is no fact of the matter about how you feel—then this can be viewed as a case of failure of reason. But ignorance of your own emotions does not automatically impugn the rationality of the emotion itself. Fears about which you are unaware might be eminently reasonable. What's unreasonable in such cases is, to some extent, *you*. And this is related to the first point: rational response to an emotion is usually predicated upon first-person awareness of the emotion. So while there are special problems in the case of emotion, there still is some sort of notable connection between the reasons for emotions and distinctively first-personal knowledge of emotions.

I conclude, then, that reasons are as such to be known: reasons are what they are at least in part because the agent whose reasons they are consciously grasps them. The Explanatory Constraint hints at this idea, because it insists that reasons for action have motivational efficacy. So does the Ownership Constraint. But your reasons not only motivate you and belong to you; unconscious drives do too. Rather, they motivate you in a very particular way, and this way has to do with first-personal knowledge. If this is indeed correct, an account of what reasons are needs to show why this is so.

The knowledge constraint

BUT BEFORE WE affirm that consequent, we need to investigate some grounds for doubting the antecedent. Do we *really* know our actions and reasons immediately and spontaneously? Perhaps it is too bold to say that *whenever* you act for a reason, you *know* what you are doing. For you might feel unsure whether you are successful in doing what you are trying to do. Suppose you are making a soufflé, your first. Because it is so easy to screw up soufflés, you would understandably be hesitant to judge that you are now indeed making a soufflé. It might flop. Of course, if all goes well, you will successfully make a soufflé; but until it's done, the jury is still out. For now, you *hope* you are making a soufflé! But you don't *know* that you are; in fact, you don't even yet believe it. So examples like this one challenge the claim that when you act for a reason, you spontaneously know what you are doing. For you might not know it at all.

Here's a second reason why it might be too bold to say that whenever you act for a reason, you *know* what you are doing. You could be wrong, even if you *don't* feel the least bit unsure whether you are succeeding, even if you fully believe that you are doing what you intend. Suppose some baseball pitcher, believing that the batter is expecting a fastball, decides to pitch a curveball in order to get a strike. Despite fully believing that he is pitching a curveball, the pitcher fails to put the appropriate spin on the ball, and the ball doesn't curve at all. It might seem very odd to say that the pitcher knows what he is doing, because he isn't even doing what he believes he is doing. (Of course, after the pitch is complete, the pitcher will probably believe that he *did* not pitch a curveball.) In this case, at least, the pitcher doesn't know what he is doing, even though he is acting for a reason.

Are these serious worries? Yes, but I think they can be overcome. There are at least three different responses to these challenges.

First, in nearly all cases where an agent who is acting for a reason is unsure or mistaken about what she is doing, the agent will still immediately know *many* of the things she is thereby doing. Consider our two examples. You may be unsure whether you are indeed making a soufflé, but you still know that you are grating cheese, that you are whipping the egg whites, that you are preheating the oven, that you are putting something in the oven, and so on. The action of making a soufflé comprises many "smaller" actions, each of which is part of making a soufflé. And there are many parts of your making a soufflé that you do know. Your skepticism about the efficacy of your action does not extend all the way to all of the parts of your action.

In the second example, the pitcher may mistakenly believe he is pitching a curveball, but he probably isn't mistaken in thinking that he is pitching, that he is playing baseball, that he is throwing the ball to (or, at least, toward) the catcher, and so on. Even if he is overconfident, even if he makes a mistake, he still knows many of the parts of what he is doing. His overconfidence about the efficacy of his action does not extend all the way to all of the parts of his action.

What does this show? It might well be misleading to say that whenever an agent acts for a reason, she immediately knows that she so acts. Still, whenever an agent acts for a reason, she immediately knows that she is doing *something* that is a part of the action (Setiya, 2007). And any acceptable theory of reasons should be able to account for this. Why is it that when you act for a reason, you immediately know that you are either 1) so acting, or, at least, 2) performing some of the actions that are parts of so acting?

That's the first of the three responses. Here's the second. Let's concede that you don't always succeed in doing what you think you are doing. You might not make a soufflé. He might not pitch that curveball. Even so, there is a sense in which you would be correct in answering the question "What are you doing?" by responding "Oh, I'm making a soufflé." For, as we're imagining it, you *are* making a soufflé. You just never make one.

We see that there is an important difference between the progressive "I was V-ing" and the perfect "I V'ed." The first does not imply the second. The tower in Pisa is falling over ... very slowly. But it may never fall over; a nuclear bomb might vaporize it first. You are now reading this book. But you may never read this book; you might lose it before you get to the end. Most action verbs function this way: the progressive can be true even if the perfect never will be. We should have some way of flagging this difference. So I will distinguish *actings* from *acts*. Actings are expressed in the imperfect or the progressive, e.g. you are eating a pizza. Acts, by contrast, are expressed in the perfect, e.g., you ate a pizza (Thompson, 2008).

How is this logical feature of grammar relevant to our present topic? The original proposal was that acting for a reason distinctively involves the agent immediately knowing what she is doing. Doubts about this proposal emerged from the examples involving lack of confidence (soufflé-making) and overconfidence (pitching a curveball). But now we can see that although you might not believe you will indeed make a soufflé, you nevertheless believe (and know) that you are mak*ing* a soufflé. That's what you're doing. Whether you succeed, of course, remains to be determined. But worries about whether you will succeed do not undercut your knowledge of what you are now *doing*. It would be perfectly correct for you to write in your diary or on your Facebook status: "I'm making my first soufflé. I hope it turns out!"

One way to see this is to think about when such actions begin. The following narration of events makes sense:

> At noon, I preheated the oven to 350, and then buttered and floured the baking dish. Next, I made the roux, and then added the milk. At 12:30, I got a little egg yolk into the mix and I had to dump it out and start all over. I was then more careful, and retraced my steps. I popped the baking dish into the oven at 1:00. I pulled it out of the oven at 1:30 and served the soufflé immediately.

Now, how long did it take me to make the soufflé? I'd say I was making the soufflé for 90 minutes, this despite the mistake I made at 12:30. The fact that I had to start over at 12:30 doesn't vitiate the description that before then I was making a soufflé. And if we were to wonder how many times was it true that I was making a soufflé, the natural answer seems to be: one, not two. Next, consider what we should say if I am instead interrupted in the kitchen at 12:35 by a request to go pick up my friend at the airport, such that I never get to finish up in the kitchen. No soufflé is ever made. And yet, nothing could be more natural than for me to describe what I was doing before I received the phone call as: making a soufflé. Hence the importance of distinguishing actings (making a soufflé) from acts (made a soufflé) (Thompson, 2011).

Thus, it should now seem more plausible to think that when you act for a reason, you immediately know what you are do*ing*, even if you don't believe that you will complete the task as intended. A theory of reasons should be able to account for why such knowledge is characteristic of those who act for reasons. So that's the second response to the expressed doubts.

Here's the third and final response. Even if there were cases in which you are acting for a reason, but you do not know that you are so acting, these cases are highly unusual. It would still be true that *typically* you immediately know what you are doing when you act for a reason. And this regularity cries out for some sort of explanation. Why is it typically true that acting for a reason involves knowing what you are doing (and, as well, the reason for which you are doing it, etc.)? The fact that there are aberrant cases where something alien interferes with our ordinary mode of knowledge does not eliminate the pressure to account for the standard case.

These three responses indicate that any account of what reasons for action are should show how we (typically) know the five conditions listed above. Thus, we should supplement our list of Constraints that an account of reasons should meet with one final desideratum: *The Knowledge Constraint*. The Knowledge Constraint requires that any satisfactory theory of reasons should be able to account for how an agent ordinarily knows 1) her reason, 2) the action, and 3) the connection between the two, all 4) immediately, and 5) spontaneously. Meeting the Knowledge Constraint will not be easy.

Constitutivism and knowledge

Do ANY OF the accounts of reasons surveyed thus far meet the Knowledge Constraint? It might seem that psychologistic accounts of reasons for action are well poised to meet the Knowledge Constraint. After all, a person ordinarily immediately knows her own psychological attitudes. So if reasons just *are* psychological attitudes, then we can see straightaway why a person would ordinarily immediately know her reasons for action.

But basic psychologistic accounts actually get us only part of the way to where we want to be. We still don't understand why someone who is acting for a reason ordinarily immediately knows *that* she is so acting. Nor yet do we grasp why she knows that *this* reason (which we've already granted she knows) is indeed *why* she is so acting; that is, we haven't accounted for how she knows that her reason "rationally causes" her action. Psychologism doesn't appear to have any distinctive advantage on this score.

Even so, it is not clear that any rival theory of reasons does either. In fact, factualist theories appear to be in even worse shape, for they seem to be unable to account even for the knowledge someone has of the reasons for which she acts. If reasons are mind-independent facts, then it's pretty hard to see how she immediately knows her reasons for action, to see why she is in a position to know them directly in a way that others are not. Hybrid theories are in better shape than factualist theories, since they conceive motivating reasons psychologistically, but even they are no better placed to meet the Knowledge Constraint than purely psychologistic theories are. So no matter how you slice it, the Knowledge Constraint seems very difficult to meet.

The most straightforward way to meet the Knowledge Constraint is to build it into an account of reasons for action *explicitly*. Unlike other bodily processes, happenings, events, and behaviors, intentional action is known as such. One might thus think that the very aim of action is to behave in a way so that you know it. Self-knowledge of a sort might be the constitutive aim of action.

This idea has great plausibility. We do indeed want to understand ourselves. When we fail to comprehend our own behavior, it can be highly disconcerting. So it makes sense to think that at least one of our aims in acting is to behave in ways that we know. I want to know what I do, and one of the best ways to accomplish this is to knowingly control what I do. It would be utterly disorienting to find myself—to my great surprise—pumping gasoline into my car. Much better to exert conscious control over what I do so that I am not caught unawares.

It thus seems sensible to think that at least *one* aim of action is this kind of self-knowledge. And it's even sensible to think that this kind of self-knowledge is a *constitutive* aim of action: it's common (though arguable) to hold that we don't just happily and coincidentally know our intentional actions; rather, this self-knowledge in part makes intentional action the very thing it is. It suffices to show that some "action" is unintentional and thus not done for a reason, if its "agent" can say sincerely that she didn't know that she was doing that.

So what would an analogous picture of practical reasons look like, on the assumption that self-knowledge of a particular sort, rather than pleasure, is the constitutive aim of action? It seems that this would imply that some consideration is a reason to act just in case acting on it would foster this sort of self-knowledge. Here's how Velleman, the leading proponent of this self-knowledge constitutivist view, puts it:

> [T]he considerations that qualify as reasons for doing something are considerations in light of which, in doing it, the subject would know what he was doing. They are, more colloquially, considerations in light of which the action would make sense to the agent. (2000, p 26)

A reason for you to act is a consideration knowledge of which would show you what you are doing. That the store has milk for sale is a reason for you to go to the store because it is in light of the fact that the store has milk that your going to the store would make sense to you. Contrast this with the case where you snap to attention, unsure of just what it is you're up to. You might come out of a daydream to find yourself walking, but with no idea for what reason. You might wonder to yourself "What *am* I doing?" But then, recalling that the store has milk might trigger the realization that you are walking to the store to get some more milk. Knowing the consideration(s) for which you are acting thus shows you what you are doing: procuring some milk. Knowing this can convert what otherwise would have been "mere activity" into what Velleman calls full-blooded intentional action.

Velleman's view of action, which understands action to be constitutively aimed at a kind of self-knowledge, is thus pretty much tailored to meet both the Ownership Constraint, and, even more clearly, The Knowledge Constraint. You know what you are doing, and indeed why you are doing it, simply because action (of the full-blooded intentional sort) is what it is only *because* it aims at this sort of self-understanding. The goal of knowing what you are doing is built into the very concept of action.

Velleman's constitutivism is thus a special version of psychologism. What grounds our reasons for action is ultimately the *aims* inherent in our agency. It's because we aim at self-knowledge that certain considerations count as reasons for action for us. But it's a version of psychologism that seeks to meet the Normative Constraint. Failing to do what you aim to do, when what you aim at is self-knowledge, is very plausibly a fault. If these constitutivists can show that failure to attain the aims of agency is what underlies failures of practical reason, then they will have produced a psychologistic account of reasons that nevertheless forges a link between reasons and normativity.

But is Velleman's version of constitutivism plausible? As with pleasure, it's an extra step to move from the thought that all action aims at self-knowledge to the thought that self-knowledge is *the* constitutive aim of action, in the sense that it supplies us with a sufficient standard of correctness that itself determines what counts as a reason for action. Here's what I mean. Let's grant that intentional action is what it is in part because agents aim to know that they are so acting. How could this supply us with a standard of correctness, in the way that truth is the standard of correctness for belief? Only by determining that an action thus known by its agent *is* correct, and an action that fails to be known by its agent (despite self-knowledge being its aim) is incorrect. For example, if in thinking that you are phoning your girlfriend you in fact call your ex-girlfriend, you won't (at first) know what you are actually doing. There's indeed a sense in which your calling your ex-girlfriend is incorrect: it isn't the action you intended, and you don't know what you are doing. The error lies in your action, rather than in your intention. Only by doing what you think you are doing can you act correctly.

But this is a very thin sense of correctness. It would seem that *anything* that you knowingly do counts as correct on this score. And so it's difficult to see how *this* sense of correctness could supply us with a guide for determining what reasons for action are (Clark, 2001). Suppose with Velleman that reasons are indeed considerations in the light of which an agent knows what she is doing. And suppose some person—call her Medea—kills her very own sons in order to hurt her husband Jason. Further, she is perfectly clear for what reason she is killing them; she is no way acting from some consideration about which she is unaware. On Velleman's self-knowledge view, Medea should thus be acting in accord with, and from, her reasons.

But it is natural to think that Medea is (or might be) acting unreasonably despite knowing full well what she is doing. Not everyone who knows what she is doing thereby acts reasonably. But if the self-knowledge view were correct, then the only sort of unreasonable action would be acting from something other than considerations in light of which the agent knows what she is doing. The self-knowledge view frowns upon acting from considerations that don't show you what you are up to, but *that* doesn't seem to be Medea's problem. Rather, one would have thought that killing your own children in order to get back at your spouse was ipso facto unreasonable. But the self-knowledge view seems not to have the resources to account for this fact. (There's also something a touch narcissistic or self-absorbed about Velleman's self-knowledge view, like what matters most of all is understanding yourself.)

Truth, by contrast, is a comparatively rich and robust standard of correctness for beliefs, in that evidence for the truth of p is, or is somehow internally related to, the reason to believe p. Believing p on weak (or no) evidence is typically to believe p for a bad (or no) reason. And there are many things that people genuinely believe without thereby believing the truth. But we don't see many genuine actions whose agents fail to attain self-knowledge; instead, it seems as if you behave in a way that you *don't* know, then you probably weren't aiming at self-knowledge in the first place. So this suggests that reasons for action have little to do with self-knowledge. The attractive part of Velleman's view is that it nicely captures the thought that those who act reasonably understand what they are doing and why they are doing it. It meets the Knowledge Constraint. But while self-knowledge may be a necessary condition for reasonable action, it seems to be far from sufficient.

Shmaction and shmagency

PERHAPS, THEN, SELF-KNOWLEDGE is not the constitutive aim of action. Perhaps the constitutive aim is something else more robust than self-knowledge, something such that actions that attain this aim really are thereby reasonable. We could canvass other specific options, one by one, to see if any of them meet this description. But some philosophers are skeptical that *any* constitutive aim strategy will reveal the nature of reasons for action. And they argue on general grounds that the constitutive aim strategy cannot work, no matter what the specific constitutive aim of action supposedly is. Let's investigate these arguments.

Suppose that full-blooded intentional action necessarily aims at A, where A can be any aim you please: pleasure, self-knowledge, self-control, autonomy, or what have you. And suppose a bit of your behavior does not in fact attain this aim A. There seem to be two possibilities. First, perhaps your behavior was indeed a full-blooded intentional action, and so was aiming at A, but did not in fact attain A. The fact that it did not meet its aim is problematic. But that's not the only possibility. Perhaps your behavior didn't even aim at A. On the second possibility, where the bit of behavior didn't even aim at A, it turns out that the bit of behavior isn't really an intentional action after all. But if it isn't really an intentional action, then it isn't defective for not attaining A. The standard of correctness embodied by the aim of A seems to govern only actions, not bits of behavior that aren't actions. Call these bits of behavior something else: *shmactions*. Actions may all aim at A, but shmactions need not. So if you don't attain A, it won't be a defect if you are shmacting rather than acting. Now why should we think that people must act rather shmact? Why think that action isn't optional in the way playing soccer is?

Sometimes this objection is expressed by focusing on the nature of agency rather than action. Rather than placing the guiding element within each and every action, we might instead find it in *capacities* or *powers* to act. If this is right, then agency itself carries with it certain constitutive commitments. Agents who meet these commitments thus qualify as rational, and, it is hoped, so do their actions. But what should we say of those who do *not* meet these commitments? Those who do not meet these commitments because they never really had these commitments in the first place turn out not to have been true agents, for, according to this constitutivist view, agents necessarily have these specific commitments—these commitments *define* agency. If they lack these commitments but are in all other respects like agents, we can instead dub them *shmagents*. Shmagents don't aim at what agents aim at, but since shmagents aren't committed to aiming at the things that agents aim at, this does not count as any failing or defect on their part. Of course, those who are indeed committed to the aims inherent in agency, but who nevertheless do not attain these aims, are thereby violating a norm or principle that governs them. But why think that those who so behave really *are* committed to the aims of agency? Why think that they are agents rather than shmagents? The fact that they do not behave like agents would seem to be some grounds for thinking that they are shmagents instead.

The shmagency challenge purports to show that the aims of agency are not mandatory. Agency does not provide reasons for everyone.

There are several possible constitutivist responses to the shmagency challenge. Here are two. First, the constitutivist might argue that agency, and thus the aims and motives that constitute agency, aren't normatively arbitrary in the way that shmagency is. Agency has a kind of importance or value that shmagency does not.

Second, the constitutivist can say that even though shmagents are conceptually possible, as a matter of fact *we* are agents. We just *do* have the aim A. Further, we don't have the option of becoming shmagents. We are *necessarily* agents. Unlike playing soccer, agency is inevitable for us. And given this fact, our actions are normatively governed by the standards of agency, such that our actions that fail to attain aim A are thereby incorrect. That it's possible for *others* to be shmagents does not change how things are for us.

David Enoch, a notable opponent of constitutivism, has developed rejoinders to both of these constitutivist moves (2006). The first move turned on the thought that agency isn't normatively arbitrary, and so there's something bad or at least less than ideal about being a shmagent rather than an agent. But Enoch points out that this is a *substantive* claim about what's valuable. Constitutivists hope to argue that we should be motivated in certain ways not because it is good to do so, as factualists do, but simply because of who we are. An argument that rests on the thought that it is good to be an agent abandons these constitutivist ambitions.

This leads us to the second move, which said that we are inevitably agents, and so constitutivism gets its grip upon *us*, even if it doesn't get its grip upon shmagents. Enoch questions what follows from the concession that agency is inevitable for us. Suppose you find yourself playing soccer. And suppose that you can't stop playing soccer, that playing soccer is for now for you inevitable. You resemble Sisyphus, I suppose. Do you now have a reason to, e.g. score goals? The aim of scoring goals is plausibly constitutive of playing soccer; if you aren't aiming to avoid a loss, you aren't really playing soccer. But Enoch points out that whether you have a *reason* to score goals depends upon you have a *reason* to play soccer, not upon whether you are *in fact* playing soccer. If playing soccer is something that you have no reason to do, then, it's unlikely that you really have a reason to score goals, even if you are condemned to play soccer. If you don't score goals, then you won't be doing what you are supposedly aiming to do. But this is a problem only if you should be playing soccer in the first place. Without some reason for playing soccer, you have no reason to score goals.

Likewise, Enoch concludes, unless you have some reason to be an agent, then you don't necessarily have a reason to pursue the aims constitutive of agency, even if it is inevitable that you *are* an agent. Inevitability thus doesn't produce normativity. And unless we are unwilling to abandon constitutivism as the ultimate account of our reasons for action, and instead argue that it's *good* to be an agent or that we have some external *reasons* to be agents, we won't be in a position to ground our commitments to agency merely in the inevitability of agency.

Enoch's challenge here may remind us of one familiar criticism of the belief-desire model of reasons for action. Some advocates of this model claim that you have a reason to V just in case you desire to V, or would desire to V under certain ideal conditions. But it's plausible that you really have a reason to V only if your desire to V is *itself* good, rational, or otherwise normatively kosher. A desire to V that is by all counts bad can't ground any reasons for action. And this is so even if the desire to V is inevitable, and can't be discarded. Whether you desire to V is one thing; whether you have reason to V is another altogether. Similarly, Enoch distinguishes between what your aims in fact are, and what aims you have reason to pursue. Whether you are an agent is one thing; whether you have reason to do pursue the aims of agency is altogether another. (Readers familiar with Moore's Open Question Argument might also note a resemblance between it and Enoch's argument.)

Constitutivism and error

CONSTITUTIVISM IS ALSO under pressure from another direction. Douglas Lavin has recently argued that constitutivism is incompatible with a widely held view about practical reason: the view that "an agent is subject to a principle only if the agent can go wrong in respect of it" (Lavin, 2004, p 425). This view Lavin calls *the error constraint*. Before we examine the supposed conflict between constitutivism and the error constraint, let's clarify the error constraint itself.

Nothing that deserves to be called a practical principle or rule can be empty or vacuous. A "rule" that said EITHER EAT MEAT OR DON'T EAT MEAT is not really a genuine practical rule at all. Rules of practical reason, should there be any, have some substance or content to them. Lavin argues that it must be at least logically possible to violate a principle of practical reason. This, he calls, the *logical* interpretation of the error constraint. This is uncontroversial.

Only slightly more controversial is the *imperatival* interpretation of the error constraint. According to this interpretation, *you* are governed by a principle or rule only if there is some way for *you* to violate the rule. To take a mundane example, consider the rule DRIVE ON THE LEFT SIDE OF THE ROAD. This rule genuinely governs you only if there's some way for you to drive on the left side of the road, and, more relevantly for present purposes, there's some way for you *not* to drive on the left side of the road. But a rule that it's impossible for you to violate isn't really a rule that binds you in any meaningful way. Consider the "rule" DON'T BISECT THE PLANET NEPTUNE. This is not a rule you can violate, although it's logically possible for someone to violate it. No matter what you in fact do, you will comply with it. And so it's not really a rule that governs you. It governs only those who *can* fail to conform to its directive. This in a nutshell is the imperatival interpretation of the error constraint.

Lavin distinguishes two versions of the imperatival interpretation: a weak version and a strong version. Both versions hold that a practical rule governs you only if you can violate it. The difference lies in the location of the source of the violation. Consider the rule SALUTE YOUR SUPERIOR OFFICER WHEN YOU SEE HER. And suppose that you failed to salute your superior officer when you saw her, only because you didn't know that the person you were seeing was indeed your superior officer. You simply confused her with someone else. Your error was a "theoretical" rather than a practical error. You failed to salute her only because at the time you were operating under a bit of misinformation.

Now the weak version of the imperatival interpretation of the error constraint says that you are governed by a rule only if it is possible for you to violate the rule, *where it does not matter why you violate it*. Violations of the rule due to errors of ignorance or due to defects in theoretical rational capacities are among those that count as relevant violations. In contrast, the strong version of the imperatival interpretation of the error constraint holds that you are governed by a rule only if it is possible for you to violate the rule, and your violating it would be a genuinely *practical* error (Lavin, 2004, p 436). The mere fact that you might not act according to the rule because you don't have a relevant bit of information is not enough to show that the rule truly governs you. The strong version holds that it governs you only if it's possible for you to violate it because you are practically defective or mistaken in some way.

Lavin illustrates this by discussing the instrumental principle of practical reason. Although it's enormously difficult to characterize exactly what the instrumental principle is, the rough idea is that you have reason to take the (necessary?) means to your (reasonable?) end. Now suppose that you have some reasonable end, such as collecting one copy of all the Galaxie 500 records ever released. But suppose you don't acquire the Galaxie 500 record *Peel Sessions* because you don't know that *Peel Sessions* even exists. You thus do not take the necessary means to your end. The weak version of the imperatival interpretation of the error constraint is consistent with holding that the instrumental principle here is a genuine principle governing you. After all, you didn't acquire a copy of *Peel Sessions*, even though it was possible for you to do so. But things are different with the strong version. If you didn't acquire *Peel Sessions* simply because you were unaware of its existence, then you have committed no *practical* error. And so if the strong version is correct, it's not clear yet whether it's possible for you to violate the instrumental principle. Merely not knowing that some action (e.g. buying *Peel Sessions*) is a necessary means to your end is not the source of any practical mistake. A practical mistake would instead be failing to take the means to your end because of, say, "terror, idleness, shyness, or depression" (Korsgaard, 1997, p 229).

Now Lavin argues that the strong version of the imperatival interpretation of the error constraint is incompatible with constitutivism. Constitutivism understands reasons for action in terms of the ideal of agency: what one has reason to do is extracted from a description of what unerring agency is. To return to the soccer analogy, a soccer player has reason to score goals because, according to the constitutivist understanding of the matter, aiming to score goals is just part of what it is to be playing soccer. Soccer players—one wants to say *real* soccer players—set the standard for playing soccer. One can easily imagine the soccer coach yelling at the lazy player "That's not how you play soccer!" Real soccer players play soccer the way it is to be played. Likewise, perfect agents are agents par excellence, acting as they have reason to act, and thus set the standard for how impure ordinary agents have reason to act.

But according to the strong version of the imperatival interpretation of the error constraint, perfect agents are not governed by any practically rational principles whatsoever. For this version holds that only those who can make practical mistakes are governed by practical principles. But perfect agents can't make practical mistakes. So we can't identify the practical principles that govern us by thinking about what pure perfect agents do. Reasons aren't constituted by the activities of ideal agents.

If Lavin is correct about this, one can't consistently be both a constitutivist and an advocate of the strong version of the imperatival interpretation of the error constraint. Of course, the would-be constitutivist can escape the problem Lavin has identified simply by retreating to a weaker version of the error constraint. Nothing about the strong version forces itself upon us. But many people, including many constitutivists, find the strong version plausible on independent grounds. It may just seem true that a principle of practical reason genuinely governs you only if there is some way for you to violate it. And if it is true, then constitutivism is in trouble.

The magic of constitutivism

CONSTITUTIVISM IS AMBITIOUS. It attempts to extract an account of reasons for action from reflection on the bare ideas of action and agency. So we shouldn't be surprised if doubts remain. Those who claim to extract reasons out of agency might remind us of those who claim to pull rabbits out of hats. You suspect that there must be a trick.

But discussing the pros and cons of constitutivism sets us up nicely to investigate one final approach to understanding reasons for action. Even if reasons can't be grounded on agency itself, perhaps constitutivists are still correct to think that reasons for action are based upon the nature of the *kind* of agent whose reasons they are. We are not merely agents; we are humans. Does this matter?

CHAPTER SEVEN

Anscombean views

Why?

IN THIS FINAL chapter, we will examine one last family of views about reasons for action. Elizabeth Anscombe was largely responsible for reviving the field of the philosophy of action in the twentieth century. And she held that the project of understanding the nature of actions is bound up with the project of understanding reasons for action. Even so, she highlighted the pointlessness of characterizing intentional action as the kind of event for which there are reasons. For there are also reasons for things other than intentional action, such as reasons for thinking that some event will take place. And we cannot helpfully pick out only the actions by saying that actions are the sort of thing for which there are *practical* reasons, because "practical reason" means just "reason for action." So we need to understand what an intentional action is in order to understand what a reason for action is. We need to grasp intentional actions and reasons for action at once.

It is difficult to summarize Anscombe's own views about what reasons for action are. Her work is notorious for being frustratingly cryptic. But she aims to shine light upon the notion an intentional action without presupposing what a reason for action is, with the goal of having an account of reasons for action *emerge* from this work.

To identify which actions are intentional, Anscombe focuses upon a special sense of the question "Why?" or "Why are you doing that?" If you ask someone why he is doing something, he might sincerely answer your question in a number of different ways. The type of answer he gives indicates whether the action about which you are asking is intentional. Certain answers show that the agent accepts the special Why-Question, indicating that the action as described is intentional, while other answers show that the agent rejects the special Why-Question, indicating that the action as described is unintentional.

Anscombe argues that this Why-Question is *rejected* if the agent can sincerely answer 1) "I didn't *know* that I am doing that" (cf. The Knowledge Constraint), 2) "I merely observe that I am doing that," 3) the answer is "evidence" for the likelihood of the thing asked about, e.g. "It has something to do with my DNA, doesn't it?", or 4) the answer states a "mental cause," e.g. "The bark of the crocodile made me flinch." In each of these cases, the action asked about is shown not to be intentional.

By contrast, the Why-Question is *accepted* if the agent sincerely mentions 5) something future, e.g. "To find the Holy Grail," 6) gives an "interpretation" of the action, e.g. "Out of vanity," 7) some bit of past history that has the idea of good or harm involved in its meaning, e.g. revenge: "Because *he* killed *my* brother!" or 8) the agent answers "No reason." In each of these cases, the action asked about *is* shown to be intentional. And Anscombe concludes that the specific answers of 5–7 each give a reason for action. A reason for action is a specific kind of answer to a specific question (Anscombe, 2000, pp 1–25).

Now each of these eight possible answers requires a lot of explication. But I'm not going to explicate them here. Contemporary Anscombeans oddly tend not to defend Anscombe's complex characterization of reasons for action. They instead draw inspiration from her methodology.

Anscombe strove to understand reasons for action by understanding what intentional action is. Specifically, she taught that actions are intentional under some descriptions but not others. In her most famous example, she describes a man who is at once moving his arm up and down, pumping water, supplying a house with water, and casting a shadow on a nearby rockery (Anscombe, 2000, p 37). The man may not know that he is casting a shadow on a nearby rockery; and if not, he is not casting the shadow there intentionally. But the man *is* operating the pump intentionally; this much is established by the fact that he immediately knows that the answer to the question "Why are you operating the pump?" is "I'm supplying the house over there with water." The man can answer the Why-Question by redescribing his action in a way that contextualizes it. Anscombeans fix their focus on the relation between these descriptions of what the man is in fact doing, rather than anything that's going on in his mind at the time of action. They look at the order that really exists among the agent's actions in order to home in on what a *reason* for action is. But *what* is this order?

The structure of action

WE HAVE SUPPOSED all along that reasons play an important role in explaining action. The Explanatory Constraint is supposed to capture this thought. Underlying this supposition is the thought that our actions *need* explaining, that our activity is not self-standing, and that we would have a better grasp on the nature of our activity if we can see how it related to something else more basic. This thought seems to be shared by psychologists, by factualists, and by those advocating hybrid theories. Psychologists and hybrid theorists hold that psychological attitudes are explanatorily prior to action, while pure factualists argue that facts or states of affairs are explanatorily prior to action.

What would justify this shared thought? Here's one idea that would: stasis is the default condition of human beings, deviations from which call for explanation.[1] If a person is doing nothing, then this requires no particular story, for, left alone, or in our natural state, we remain idle. Fundamentally, we are at rest. When we *do* things, however, then this prompts the sort of puzzlement that can be relieved only with an explanation. Actually, there are two questions here we should distinguish. First, why is someone acting at all, rather than remain idle? And second, why is she acting as she is, rather than acting in some other way? Answers to both of these questions, it may seem, must be in terms of something other than action, something that is more fundamental than action, such as facts or psychological attitudes. Like I said, that's one idea.

Once expressed, though, this idea should strike us as implausible, or at least as not obviously true. For it is at least as plausible to think that human beings are by default or naturally 1) active as opposed to idle, and 2) active in some particular ways as opposed to others. If it's wrong to think that *objects* naturally come to rest when there is no external force imposed upon them, then it would be no more correct to think that human beings are naturally idle if no external force is imposed upon them.

This is so for two different reasons. First, we shouldn't assume that human beings are naturally static as opposed to active. Perhaps it is inactivity rather than activity that requires explanation. Humans are, on the whole, a pretty busy bunch. Second, we shouldn't assume that because *some* of our actions require explanation, all do. There may be specific ways that people naturally act, while other ways of acting are deviations from what's natural and so indeed call for explanation.

None of this is meant to suggest that actions, or some actions, are entirely immune to explanation. Nearly everything is subject to explanation, and actions are no exception. Even so, we ought not presume that actions are any *more* in need of explanation than are facts, or values, or psychological attitudes, or anything else. It would be a mistake to overlook the possibility that these other things are (sometimes) to be explained in terms of action, rather than (only) the other way around.

What does this all imply? Let's again acknowledge the fact that reasons for action have a certain kind of explanatory function— reasons are that for which we act—and that any plausible account of reasons for action must accommodate this feature. But we should now be able to see clearly that this fact does not establish that reasons for actions must be something pre- or non-agential. In particular, reasons need not be static.

The most obvious alternative idea to explore is that reasons for actions are dynamic. The dynamism of the *explanans* (the thing explained) would then be matched by the dynamism of the *explanandum* (the thing doing the explaining). Of course, this idea doesn't itself tell us very much about what an action *is* or about *what* can be a reason for action.

To make progress on that front, let's focus upon the *distinctions* among the kinds of things for which there are reasons, and how this might be related to differences among the kinds of reasons themselves. We shouldn't assume that reasons for action are *exactly* like reasons for other things, such as reasons for belief or judgment.

Features of the logical structure of what is judged can constrain what is eligible to serve as a reason for judgment. Formalization can obscure this fact. When thinking about reasons for judgment, we easily slip into talk about reasons for judging p. Likewise, when thinking about reasons for action, we easily slip into talk about reasons for V-ing. In and of itself, this is fine. But dwelling upon these variables can make us forget about important features of the values of these variables. The one-letter variable p does not take simple items as its values. It instead takes propositions (or complete thoughts or sentences or states of affairs) whose internal structure comprises an object and a concept (or a subject and a predicate), related to each other in a particular way. *This* structure is complex. And, for all we know, the fact that propositions have the complex structure that they do bears upon why there *are* reasons for judging that p in the first place, and, more importantly for present purposes, upon what shape the reasons for these judgments take. Davidson (1986) once wrote that nothing could be a reason for a belief except another belief. His grounds for writing this were various, but perhaps one of them is the thought that a belief (or its contents) has the correct structure to serve as a reason for another belief.

Like beliefs, actions have a particular structure. And here I want to evaluate a hypothesis analogous to Davidson's: nothing can be a reason for action except another action (or something related to action). If reasons and the things for which they have reasons have the same structure, then the most obvious candidate for a reason for an action is: an action. But how plausible is this?

Naïve action theory

MICHAEL THOMPSON, THE leading contemporary Anscombean, also focuses on the "Why?" question. He argues that the most common way to explain one action is in terms of another action (Thompson, 2008). Some intuitively plausible examples:

"Why are you reading that book?"
—"I'm learning about reasons."

"Why are you traveling to Italy?"
—"I'm visiting my mother there."

"Why are you breaking those eggs?"
—"I'm making an omelet."

In these and countless other cases, one action is offered as a reason for another.[2] This "naive action theory" Thompson expressly defends opposes a supposedly more sophisticated view according to which reasons for action are always best represented psychologically:

"Why are you reading that book?"
—"I *want* to learn about reasons."

"Why are you traveling to Italy?"
—"I *want* to visit my mother there."

"Why are you breaking those eggs?"
—"I *want* to make an omelet."

Sometimes you explain what you are doing by noting, not what else you are also doing, but what you *want* to do. And sophisticated action theory holds that this is the canonical way to express most reasons for action.

Thompson doesn't deny the propriety of the sort of explanation emphasized by the sophisticates. Sometimes we *do* explain actions by citing what we want. But he holds that sophisticated action explanations are in a certain sense dependent upon the success of naive action explanation. Naive action explanations are primary, and the sophisticated ones are to be understood as variants of these.

Consider again the question "Why are you breaking those eggs?" It doesn't make much difference whether one replies "I'm making an omelet" or "I want to make an omelet." Both are true, and both sound natural (Anscombe, 2000, p 40) Now consider the question "Why are you *buying* those eggs?" Here it may sound more natural to reply "I want to make an omelet" rather than "I'm making an omelet." That is, it sounds odd to say "I'm making a omelet" while you are still in the dairy section of the grocery store.

You might think that you aren't making an omelet just *yet*. This oddity may appear to force us to choose between explaining the egg-buying psychologistically ("I want to make an omelet") or by putting the rationalizing action clearly in the future ("I will make an omelet"). And unease with explaining the present by means of the future can make it appear that the psychologistic explanation is the only legitimate one available. This all suggests that the sophisticated theory is correct.

But often we can eliminate the oddity by inserting an adverb indicating the future time at which the action will be going on: "I am making omelets *tonight*." The verb remains in the present tense, but the adverb indicates when the action will be more fully underway. The action of making omelets is only beginning to unfold there in the aisle of the grocery store. The present-progressive-and-future-adverb is one way to unite what's going on in the present and what will be going on in the future. Something similar is going on with expressions like "I am about to make on omelet" and "I am going to make an omelet." The agent depicts herself as now in the early stages of a lengthy process. Actions take time, so the fact that the end of the omelet-making will be going on tonight does not rule out the possibility that the early stages of the omelet-making are going on right now.

Thompson proposes that we think of psychologistic explanations as *further* variants of these bridging expressions. There's not a significant difference between saying "I'm making an omelet later" and "I intend to make an omelet," even though the surface language of only the latter refers explicitly to a state of mind. Someone who *intends* to make an omelet is already *doing* many of the things necessary for the creation of the omelet: buying the cheese and eggs, washing the pan, turning on the heat—or perhaps just avoiding doing things that would interfere with successful omelet-making, such as throwing all of the eggs in the house at the neighbor's pesky dog. If she is now knowingly sabotaging all hope of making an omelet, then it just is not true that she intends to make an omelet. And what's true for intending also seems to be true for many instances of wanting: someone who really wants (and not merely wishes) to make an omelet is already inhabiting at least the earliest stages of producing it.

We might doubt this on the grounds that it seems possible to want and even intend to make an omelet *before* one has taken *any* of the steps of omelet-making. We want to say: intending is one thing, doing another. To see why this doubt is misguided, we need to get clearer about the nature of intentional action itself. Remember in 6.2 we distinguished between actings and acts. Right now you are reading this book. But you have not read it (unless you are now re-reading it). And you may never read it: you may lose it before you finish, or you may get bored with it and set it aside, or you may give it to a friend who needs it right away, or you may just need to fuel the fire somehow. There's a difference, then, between "Agnes was V-ing" and "Agnes V-ed," for the former does not imply the latter. Agnes can start doing something without ever finishing it. We are calling the former kind of action an *acting*, and the latter kind of action an *act*.

There are several substantive differences between actings and acts. For most values of the variable, "Agnes is V-ing" will be true (if ever true) for a stretch of time. If Agnes is, say, shopping for Halloween candy, this does not happen in the twinkling of an eye. There is no particular point or moment in time such that she was shopping for Halloween candy at only that point in time, but neither before nor after. Rather, her shopping for Halloween candy has some duration. For instance, it might be true that Agnes was shopping for Halloween candy right after she left work but before she picked up her dry cleaning. Maybe this took about a half an hour. Usually, the temporal boundaries on actings will be very vague: it is almost always far from obvious when they begin. There seems to be an element of arbitrariness in any judgment about exactly when you started e.g. cleaning your office.

But it's a characteristic feature of many (if not most) intentional actions that typically there *is* a fairly clearly identifiable point when they are over. If you are writing an email message to your sister, it may be unclear exactly when you began. Was it while you were reading her last message to you? While you were thinking about what you might say in reply? While you were opening up your email software? While you were typing something in the subject line? When you stopped deleting everything you typed in your false starts? But your writing does not go on forever: at some point—possibly, when you hit send—you stop writing an email message to your sister, and it is only at the moment true that you *have written* an email message to your sister. The perfective "Agnes has bought some Halloween candy" or "You have written an email message to your sister" is true just as the acting is over and done with, but not before.

Thus there is no time t such that at t it was *both* true that "Agnes is buying Halloween candy" and that "Agnes has bought Halloween candy"—not unless she is buying Halloween candy *again*, or buying *more* candy. For she stops buying some Halloween candy as soon as she has bought Halloween candy. To be sure, instantaneous actions are different. The great majority of actions, however, are not instantaneous. It would be a mistake, though, to think that the expression "Agnes has bought some Halloween candy" means nothing more than that although Agnes was buying some Halloween candy, she no longer is. For it might instead be the case that while at some point she was indeed buying some Halloween candy, she never did buy any. The perfective expression says not only that an agent was V-ing and no longer is; but also that she successfully V-ed.

Now, what has all this to do with *reasons*? The structure of actions is related to the form that reasons for action can take. Let's examine this structure more closely. "Agnes is buying some Halloween candy" is an acting that comprises multiple parts. There are many different ways to be buying some Halloween candy, and there is probably no set of necessary conditions for buying Halloween candy. Agnes might drive to the grocery store or walk to the convenience store. She might select the chocolates or the pixie sticks. She might pay with cash or with her credit card. And so on.

What is true of "Agnes is buying some Halloween candy" is also true of each of its parts. First, there are multiple ways to walk to the store, to select the pixie sticks, and to pay with cash. She might walk to the store by going north, then east; or by going east, then north. She might lumber, plod, meander, stroll, or jog, or some combination thereof. She might break a $50 bill, or empty her change jar, or minimize the total number of coins and bills to exchange hands. Second and relatedly, each of the parts of buying Halloween candy itself comprises multiple parts. In paying with cash, she might plunge her hand into her purse, feel around for her wallet, pull it out, open the change container, give the cashier the correct coins, close the change container, open up the billfold, give the cashier a $20 bill, wait while the cashier counts out her $8 in change, put the $8 in the billfold, replace the wallet in her purse, and throw away the receipt at her first opportunity. Or she might pay with cash in some other combination of ways. The point is: each of these actings comprises several smaller actings.

We can remain agnostic on the difficult question whether actings can be infinitely subdivided into other actings; perhaps there is always some smallest acting, or perhaps actions are instead *practical fractals*.[3] Either way, actings are *typically* not atomic points—they generally have a rich internal structure.

Let's look at the same subject matter from a different vantage point. An action such as "Agnes is buying some Halloween candy" is itself often a part of some still larger action. For instance, "Agnes is buying some Halloween candy"—complex as it is—is just one part of "Agnes is hosting a costume party," an action that has very many parts. And the action of "Agnes is hosting a costume party" may be part of a larger action still. It is highly unlikely that—and perhaps it's even incoherent to think—that there is *always* a larger action. As Aristotle observed, if we do everything for the sake of something else, with the process going on to infinity, our pursuits would be in vain. Even so, most actions are embedded within other larger ones, and embed other smaller ones.

I have spoken of larger actions, but talk of "larger" obscures an important distinction. One action might be larger than another in the way that "Agnes is buying some Halloween candy" is related to "Agnes is walking to the convenience store": the latter is not sufficient for the former; rather, the former encompasses the latter and more. There is more to buying Halloween candy than merely walking to the store. We might say that "walking to the convenience store" is *a proper part* of "buying some Halloween candy." This is the relation emphasized by Thompson.

Another way one action might be larger than another, emphasized by (Ford, n.d.), is by being more *general* than the other. Taking the Concorde is (or was) one of many different particular ways of crossing the ocean. And taking the Concorde *is* sufficient for crossing the ocean; it's not merely some proper part. We might say that "taking the Concorde" is a *specification* of "crossing the ocean." "Crossing the ocean" is larger than "taking the Concorde," in the sense of being a more general description of it.

Thus we have both the part-whole relation and the specific-general relation, each of which most actions enter into. In both cases, there are important temporal connections between the actions so related. Whenever the proper part (or the specification) is under way, so too is the whole (or the more general). So in the circumstances we have already imagined, when Agnes is meandering northeasterly, she is thereby and then also 1) walking to the convenience store (specific-general), and 2) buying some Halloween candy (part-whole). Each of these would be predictable responses to the question, "For what reason are you meandering north-easterly?" And each of these "larger" actions is in progress as she is meandering northeasterly. They overlap temporally.

We now can answer a challenge posed earlier. I proposed that if one is intending to V, then it's not wrong to say now that one is V-ing. But this appeared incorrect, as it seems possible to decide to V later without taking any of the steps that constitutes V-ing. For instance, I might now intend to watch a documentary about whales next week. But it's not now true that I'm watching a documentary about whales next week, is it?

And yet, there are many ways to watch a documentary about whales. Some of these ways are unintentional: aiming to watch a crime thriller, you might step into the wrong theater at the multiplex, and instead be transfixed by some display of marine life. But the most common way of intentionally watching a documentary about whales begins with *intending to watch a documentary about whales*. This is usually the first step, and so may rightly be characterized as itself part of the action. More generally, intending to V is *part* of intentionally V-ing. One might feel reluctant to accept this point if one is wedded to a Cartesian view of the mind, according to which there is a sharp break between *action*, which involves only the moving around of matter, and *thinking*, which involves only the operations of some immaterial substance, with never the two overlapping. But mental action is in fact action, and mental action is at least often part of intentional action. So there is no bar to characterizing intending to V as itself part of intentionally V-ing.

This result may seem more intuitive if we focus on the role of deliberation. Suppose you are deliberating about how to get your things from your old apartment to your new one. Getting your things from one place to another is a complicated process. There are many smaller activities that collectively constitute it. But common to most of these sets of activities that collectively constitute it is the step of *deliberating about how to get your things from one place to another*. It is commonplace to observe that deliberating is itself an action. What's less often understood is that deliberating about how to V is itself an often crucial part of V-ing. The parts of complex intentional activities, then, are not limited to the movements of the muscles. And what goes for deliberating also goes for intending, wanting, and the other practical operations of the mind.

So naïve action theory does not flat out deny that psychological attitudes can be thought of as reasons for action. In some circumstances, they can be. Rather, naïve action theory views the significance of this fact in a particular way. Wanting to act can be a reason just insofar as acting itself can be a reason. We understand the former only because we understand the latter. Sophisticated action theory isn't *completely* wrong; rather, the grain of truth it contains depends upon the prior truth of naïve action theory.

Now attend again to the idea that if one thing is a reason for a second thing, then the two things have the same structure. We now can see more clearly how an action can be a reason for another action, although the word "another" in the phrase "another action" is misleading. If you are melting some butter because you are making some cookies, the second action is your reason for the first. But the action of melting some butter is *neither* strictly identical to *nor* wholly different from the action of making some cookies—instead, the one is a proper part of the other. The rational relation between the two actions relies upon this deeper unity. We could put the point somewhat mysteriously: the two actions are the same and yet different.

Yet this cryptic thought should seem a little familiar. In Chapter 1, we saw that Plato thought that Reason unifies different parts of the soul that might otherwise conflict with each other. Reason tends to the entire soul, bringing its various tendencies and impulses in harmony with each other. In a soul ruled by Reason, the soul is not at war with itself; rather, the several parts of the soul are brought together so that they are rightfully viewed by the agent as all belonging to *herself*. Nothing she does strikes her as alien. Reason makes her *one* rather than many.

The most straightforward way for different *actions* to be thus unified is for the one to be either a proper part of, or specification of, the other. Meandering northeast can be, in certain circumstances, walking to the convenience store, which itself can be, in certain circumstances, at least part of buying Halloween candy. You thus might be meandering northeast *for the reason* that you are walking to the convenience store, which you are doing *for the reason* that you are buying Halloween candy. Conceived this way, reasons for action are simply other ways of characterizing the same action that show their further point.

This suggests a particular way to spell out the difference between an agent in whom Reason rules, and other sorts of agents. While all agents may be doing lots and lots of different things, only in the case of the agent in whom Reason rules are these various actings highly unified, related to one another in either the part-whole or the general-specific way. The irrational agent, by contrast, does many things that frustrate or are at odds with his other activities. The irrational agent is intentionally do*ing* many things which he never really does.

Actions and facts

I HAVE ALREADY briefly explained how naïve action theory can account for what's seems to be true about psychologism: *wanting* to act can function as a reason for action only because *action itself* can be a reason for action. But can naïve action theory also account for what's seems to be true about factualism? There's something perfectly appropriate about saying things like "My reason for buying poison is that there are rats in my yard." And "that there are rats in my yard" is no *action* of mine, not in any sense of the word. It seems to be a reason for action that *isn't* itself an action. Doesn't this show rather simply and vividly that naïve action theory is false?

Here is as good a time as any to note that Thompson and other Anscombeans don't think that actions (and wanting to act) are the *only* kind of reason for action that there is. At least some also think that social practices can underwrite actions. For instance, your reason for helping a friend move her sofa into her new apartment might be: you promised her that you would. The practice of promising can thus be the source of a reason for your action. Not every reason for action is thus another *particular* action. In the case of a practice, it is something *general*. (Still, though, on Thompson's view particular actions are the *sine qua non* of reasons.)

But the challenge posed by factualism is very different. Factualism regards particular facts, not general practices, as reasons for action.

The fact that there are rats in my yard is nothing general. It's a garden-variety particular fact, *literally* even.

To meet the factualist challenge, we need to think more about how a consideration like "that there are rats in my yard" is or is related to a reason for buying poison. "That there are rats in my yard" can be a reason for buying poison only if buying poison enables me to *do* something about the rats in my yard. More specifically, "that there are rats in my yard" is a reason for buying poison, because, if I buy poison, I can thereby kill the rats in my yard. So it seems that the *real* reason for buying poison is that I am thereby killing the rats in my yard. It's the fact that I can say "I'm buying poison because I'm killing the rats in my yard" that makes the fact there are rats in my yard at all relevant for whether I have reason to buy poison. Unless I can kill the rats in my yard by buying poison, the mere fact that there are rats in my yard—though a nightmare—is not itself a reason for me to buy poison. In fact, it would be a very random thing to do!

Thus a consideration like "there are rats in my yard" is not the entire reason for which I am buying poison; rather, it is an ingredient of my reason. The full reason for buying poison is "I'm killing the rats in my yard." Now pragmatics permit me to draw my listener's attention to the most informative element of the full reason, and so I may mention only the bit about the rats in my yard. But my full reason for buying poison is not merely that there are rats in my yard, but that I'm thereby killing the rats in my yard.[4] So naïve action theory appears to have the resources to account for what seems plausible about factualism.

Keeping score

HOW WELL DOES this Anscombean view meet our various Constraints? If the reason for some particular action is a larger action of which it is a part or a means, then the reason contextualizes the first action, showing how it fits in a larger pattern and how it makes sense in the life of the agent. Contextualization is a familiar form of explanation. Often we explain something by articulating how it plays a role in a bigger scheme. When something fails to be appropriately contextualized, it often appears to be ad hoc, surd, or—well—irrational. Contextualization puts things in order. (Recall here the Platonic emphasis on harmony.) This style of explanation is, of course, not a form of efficient causal explanation. But the Explanatory Constraint demands only that we show how reasons can explain the actions for which they are reasons, not that we show how reasons can efficiently cause these actions.

We might be tempted to think that only efficient causation will do. Pressure to think this comes from arguments like the multiple reasons argument, which we encountered in Chapter 2. You can act for one of your reasons rather than for another of your reasons. You can act some way *because* you have a *particular* reason. An account of reasons should be able to accommodate this. Fortunately, Thompson's theory can. I am now writing this sentence for the reason that I am writing this book, not for the reason that I enjoy writing sentences that illustrate their very point, although that *is also* a reason I have. More generally, one can be A-ing because one is B-ing, not because one is C-ing—even though one is C-ing too. So the multiple reasons argument does not tell against naïve action theory.

But even characterizing the kind of explanation that reasons provide as contextualization is a bit too weak. We can approach the explanatory relation between actions and its reasons from another angle. Actions are not, or are not *merely*, behaviors with special causes. The standards of goodness of an action show us something about what action itself *is*. One place we find this thought expressed is in Kant's ethics. The moral worth of an action, he taught us, depends upon considerations concerning its internal structure. There is an important sense in which charging your customers correctly in order to preserve your reputation is not the same action as charging your customers correctly in order to act honestly, and this is why the two actions are not morally equivalent. We might even orthographically signify this with hyphens: charging-your-customers-accurately-in-order-to-preserve-your-reputation ≠ charging-your-customers-accurately-in-order-to-act-honestly.

It might be tempting to disagree, holding instead that all we have here are two different tokens of the same action, albeit each with a different purpose, and that the difference in value stems wholly from the nature of something other than the action itself, such as the purpose of the action. On a view like this, the value of the action is *imported from* the value of some non-action (e.g. the purpose), an action that is otherwise the same in the two cases. The action is, as it were, only externally related to what makes it good.

This temptation might be bolstered by the fact that in *both* cases it very well may be true that when you charge your customers accurately, you really do preserve your reputation. The latter happens "by means of" the former, whether or not the latter is your actual purpose. So it might seem that in both cases the action and the results are the same; the only difference is in your intention, a difference that is only something internal and psychological, not a difference that alters at all "what you do" or "what happens."

But this is wrong. Korsgaard (2008, p 227) helps us to see why:

> Giving a description or explication of the action, and giving a description or explication of the reason, are the same thing. The logos or maxim which expresses the reason is a kind of description of the action, and could be cited in response to the question: *what is he doing?* just as easily as it can in response to the question *why is he doing that?* Indeed—to make one last appeal to our ordinary practices—their view explains why in ordinary language these questions are pretty much equivalent. For the demand for justification can as easily take the form: *what are you doing?* or more aggressively and skeptically *what do you think you are doing?* as it can *why are you doing that?* The reason for an action is not something that stands behind it and makes you want to do it: it is the action itself, described in a way that makes it intelligible.

The question "Why are you doing that?" can usually also be asked by the questions "What are you doing?", "What do you think you are doing?", or—still more aggressively—"What the hell do you think you are doing?" An appropriate response to a request to justify what you are doing is to describe what you are doing in another way. You say that you're not just napping; you're taking a study break. You say that you're not just charging your customers the correct price; you're building up your store's reputation. Re-describing what you are doing in these ways just *is* to give your reasons for doing it. If this is correct, then reasons explanations do not merely contextualize the actions that they explain, as though the reasons were the rest of the scenery on action's stage. Rather, reasons *explicate* the actions for which they are reasons. The Explanatory Constraint thus seems to be met.

Consider next the Knowledge Constraint. The Knowledge Constraint says that a satisfactory account of reasons for action should at least be compatible with, or even outright account for, the fact that one knows straightaway and spontaneously one's reasons for action. You don't usually have to infer or figure out your own reasons for acting in the way that you need to figure out the reasons of others. Rather, you know your own reasons for actions in much the same way as you know your actions themselves.

Now if reasons for action just *are* other actions, then it's no wonder that you know your *reasons* for what you are doing in the same way that you know *what* you are doing. For instance, you know straightaway that you are reading this sentence. Likewise, you know that you are reading this chapter. Now, if you are reading this sentence for the reason that you are reading this chapter, then you know your *reason* for reading this sentence in the same way that you know *that* you are reading this sentence itself. We generally know our reasons for acting because we generally know what we are doing. Of course, we would still like to understand better just how it is we straightaway know what we are intentionally doing. Philosophers of action have various stories to tell about that. But however that question gets resolved, presumably the question about how we know our *reasons* for what we are doing can be resolved in the same way, if reasons are actions themselves.

You also know the *connection* between what you are doing and your reason for doing it. It's not as though that you know that, on the one hand, you are reading this sentence, and on the other hand, that you are reading this chapter—but are in the dark that the latter is indeed your reason for the former. You know this connection as well as you know either bit on its own. In fact, *unless* you in some sense know that you are reading this sentence for the reason that you are reading this chapter, then it is just isn't true that you are reading this sentence *for* the reason that you reading this chapter. There would have to be some other style of explaining what you are up to, perhaps one best supplied by a psychoanalyst. The Anscombean view, then, is well positioned to account for the distinctive way we know our own reasons for actions, and so can meet the Knowledge Constraint quite naturally.

Next consider the Ownership Constraint. The Ownership Constraint says that a satisfactory account of reasons should show how your reasons for actions are indeed *your* reasons, rather than alien considerations imposed upon you by wholly external standards. A reason for you to do something is a reason you (in some sense) can identify with.

Now if your reasons for acting are just other actions of yours already under way, then clearly you are already engaged with your reasons. Agnes's reason for walking to the convenience store, remember, is that she is buying some Halloween candy. Buying some Halloween candy is not alien to her; it's something she is already doing. She won't feel the need to complain: why should I care about buying some Halloween candy?—for buying some Halloween candy is something she is already up to. This is not to deny that there are times when we question whether the projects we are in the middle of are really worth pursuing. Ethical and other practical questions may still loom large. But the default stance is to be engaged with the activities one is in the midst of. So the Anscombean view also seems to meet the Ownership Constraint.

The Anscombean view is probably most vulnerable to failure in meeting the Normative Constraint. As with psychologistic theories of reasons, it can seem that naïve action theory fails to capture fully the critical dimension of reasons for action. Return to the case of the Heartless Husband. We would like to be able to say that he has reason to treat his wife nicely. But is it true? Is there some activity that he is already engaged in, such that treating her more nicely is either a means to (or part of) it? It is not obviously so. Perhaps the Anscombean view cannot account for the normativity of the reasons we pretheoretically think people have.

Activity and normativity

There are multiple replies to this worry available to the Anscombean. One option, of course, is just to accept this implication, as did Williams. That is, we might reply by acknowledging that cases like that of the Heartless Husband are hard but extreme cases, and by confessing that while we can correctly condemn him in all kinds of ways, it would be a mistake to accuse him of also being blind to his reasons. The wicked may be perfectly reasonable. This is the line that (Vogler, 2002) takes. An Anscombean, Vogler argues that in the absence of a theological context it is a mistake to hold that the vicious are *ipso facto* acting contrary to reason. This tack requires scaling back the Normative Constraint. Failing to respond to one's reasons is still a *practical* defect. But many ethical defects aren't defects of practical reason. Evil is not itself a form of irrationality.[5]

Let's call this *the pessimistic response*. The pessimistic response is not the only possible reply. Here is an *optimistic* strategy that the Anscombean might instead pursue. We could show that even the Heartless Husband has a reason to be nicer to his wife, if we can show that he is already engaged in some activity that would be furthered by his being nicer to her. For such an activity would then be his reason for treating her more nicely. But what activity could this plausibly be?

There are several optimistic options here. First, Aristotle argued that *eudaimonia* (happiness) is an activity. We should construe this claim quite literally (Brown 2006). Eudaimonia is not a mere outcome, result, or goal of other activities—although there is a sense in which it might also be each of these. Eudaimonia is an activity itself constituted by smaller actions. It's hard to express this thought about eudaimonia in English. We do not say things like "I'm happying," although we can say "I'm flourishing." Even so, "flourishing" does not usually come to mind as an example of an intentional action. Slightly better might be "I'm living the (good) life." While *being* alive is not an activity, living is. And if one is living well, then one is, as I shall say, eudaimon-ing.

Aristotle argued not only that eudaimonia is an activity, but also that it is an activity that each and every one of us is engaged in, in the sense that we are at least aiming at eudaimonia. He claims that we do everything for the sake of eudaimonia. Most of us, however, do not completely realize or instantiate this activity. We try; we fail. We have different ideas about how to succeed; most of them are incorrect. But we are alike in that we all are (or at least were?) eudaimon-ing, even though in the end so few of us successfully eudaimon-ed.

This thought of Aristotle's might appear to echo the central claim of psychological egoism. The psychological egoist says that everyone really always acts so as to benefit herself, even when it might appear that some people act instead for selfless reasons. Earlier we saw why this view isn't very plausible. Is Aristotle's claim any different?

One reason to think so is that Aristotle conceives his claim as one upon which everyone agrees. He doesn't present it as anything controversial. In fact, he thinks that people who disagree about all sorts of other things at least agree to *this*. And it's not only Aristotle who thinks that everyone aims at eudaimonia. Just about *all* the ancient Greek philosophers thought that everyone aims at eudaimonia; the only exceptions are the Cyrenaics, who held that people should aim at pleasure *instead* of eudaimonia. The psychological egoist, by contrast, realizes that he is promoting a view of human nature that many others regard as cynical and wrongheaded. He knows he is saying something that seems counterintuitive. So we should hesitate lumping Aristotle in with the psychological egoists.

A second important difference is that psychological egoists usually hold that people frequently *succeed* in reaching their supposed goal. For instance, if you vote in the upcoming election, the psychological egoist will likely note that when you vote, you feel good about yourself, and that in voting you aimed at feeling good about yourself by voting. It would be odd to insist that you had this as your underlying aim if you succeed in achieving this goal only rarely. You'd think you'd learn better. Rather, the psychological egoist tends to think that often we really do achieve our self-interested aims.

The same cannot be said for the goal of eudaimonia. Although everyone aims at eudaimonia, few in fact completely succeed. Eudaimonia is not the sort of goal that one achieves on one day, and then aims at a second time the next day. Eudaimonia is instead the kind of goal that can be predicated only of one's life as a whole. Just as a basketball team doesn't win a minute or a half but only an entire game, so too one attains eudaimonia not in a day or a year but only in one's entire life. So unlike what the psychological egoist means by "happiness," "benefit," or "interest," eudaimonia is a goal one continually aims at in part because one can never rest having finally attained it.

If this is correct, then the Heartless Husband has a reason to be nicer to his wife, if treating his wife more nicely is indeed a part of his living a happy life, and he is already in the midst of doing that. This, of course, is a substantive question, and it's not perfectly obvious that treating his wife more nicely really *would* be a part of his living a successful, happy life. But it's plausible that this is really so, and that the Heartless Husband is frustrating his own pursuing a happy life by treating her cruelly. That is, it's plausible that he is currently engaged in a life that's practically self-defeating. He would live more eudaimonly, it may seem, if he were to treat her well. This is the first optimistic option.

One might wonder how this option is substantively any different from Williams' own proposal. Williams grants that the Heartless Husband has a reason to treat his wife more nicely if, but only if, he *cares* or *is motivated by* any thing that would be served by treating his wife more nicely. And though unlikely, it seemed possible that he might *not* care about any such thing. The Anscombean view differs from Williams' in that it relates reasons to the agent's activity rather than to his cares and motives. But can an agent be involved in an activity that he neither cares about nor is motivated to pursue? That is: if it makes any sense to characterize the Heartless Husband as eudaimon-ing, isn't he also *motivated* to be eudaimoin-ing? Or, contrapositively, if the Heartless Husband isn't motivated to be eudaimon-ing, then he just *isn't* eudaimon-ing, despite what the ancients say.

Perhaps it *is* implausible that everyone is always eudaimon-ing. But in order to defend her view, the Anscombean need not claim that everyone is. This brings us to the second optimistic option. Recall from 7.2 the thought that just because *some* of your activities require explanation, it's not obvious that all of them do so. And just as you do not need a reason for eudaimon-ing, so too could there be other activities for which you need no reason. And your *other* activities would be adequately rationalized if you can hook each of them up with one of *these*.

Let me illustrate with a comparatively uncontroversial case. Suppose you give your sick child some aspirin. For what reason? Because you are taking care of her. Giving her some aspirin is a specification of taking care of her. Now one might ask: for what reason are you taking care of your child? But this is a puzzling question. I mean, there *are* things you can say to explain why you are taking care of your child. But in another way, it can seem that this is just a dumb question. What kind of question is "for what reason are you taking care of your child?"! Taking care of one's child is just what a person who has a child *does*. What requires explanation is why a person who has a child *isn't* taking care of her.

Of course, there are plenty of *reasons-why* you are taking care of your child. Such reasons might concern genes, evolution, culture, guilt, love, religion, and a whole host of other possibilities. No doubt these reasons are very complex. But we aren't concerned here with the reasons *why* things happen, but the reasons *for* which we act. Is there a reason for which you are taking care of your child? It's not clear that there is.

There thus seems to be an asymmetry here. What justifies the asymmetry is that taking care of one's offspring is somehow the *sort* of thing creatures like us do. Taking care of your offspring isn't something that you need a reason *for*, not in the way that you need a reason for, say, breaking some eggs. The reason for which *you* take care of *your* child is, if anything at all, nothing but the reason for which *people* take care of their own children. We don't need to supplement our anthropology with your biography in order to grasp your reasons for taking care of your child. It's instead perfectly natural.

This use of "nature" and "natural," of course, will raise hackles and trigger alarm bells. So let's not rest too heavily on the idea of the natural. All that's needed here is for the chain of practical reasoning to arrive at a V-ing, such that your V-ing doesn't need to be connected to some *further* thing in order to be vindicated. Eudaimon-ing, for one, needs no further vindication. But neither do many other kinds of activities. Anscombe herself notes that no one needs to surround the activities of eating and drinking with further explanations in order for us to see their point (2000, p 73). And there are many such activities, some of which are perhaps grounded biologically, some of which are grounded socially and culturally.[6]

These actions that need no further *action* to rationalize them can be given what Anscombe called a *desirability characterization* (2000, p 72). Anscombe points out that Aristotle usually portrayed chains of practical reasoning as terminating in some statement about the desirability of the action. Examples include characterizing an action as "suitable" or "pleasant."[7] Taking care of your own child is suitable or fitting. (Sometimes, it's also pleasant or otherwise pretty cool.) Of course, whether some action really is suitable or pleasant or otherwise desirable may be sensibly challenged; those who challenge the propriety of the parental roles of the traditional family are hardly unintelligible. But *this* challenge would not be about the validity of the practical reasoning involving such a claim, but is addressed to the truth of one of the "premises." It would be an argument for the conclusion that some *other* social arrangement is suitable, fitting, or appropriate, not an argument about whether there's anything good about doing what's suitable.

In any case, if some action can be given a desirability characterization, the action is shown to be good in some way. This way may be rather minor: perhaps all that is established is that acting in some way would be mildly pleasant. It certainly need not be *ethically* good. But this is still more robust than the anemic sense in which Davidson's primary reasons justify the actions for which they are reasons, the sense that the action is desired by the agent in question.

Not all tokens of intentional actions, however, can be given desirability characterizations. Most readers of Anscombe are confused about her views on this matter. She *is* well known for arguing that there are constraints on what can be intelligibly wanted. Consider someone who says, "I want a saucer of mud." Anscombe argues that we don't understand what such a person really wants, not without further contextualization or information. What does he want it *for*? Perhaps he just wants to *own* something. Perhaps he wants to see if we will fulfill an odd request. Perhaps he is making a point to bolster a philosophical position. Any of these things are certainly possible and intelligible. But absent such an explanation, we don't yet understand what the man is saying, because we don't see how such an object is desirable. Wanting objects is not always intelligible (Anscombe, 2000, pp 70–1).

But nearly no one registers what *else* Anscombe says about the constraints on what can be intelligibly wanted. In the penultimate section of *Intention*, she writes:

> It is different with a proposed action. My remarks about "wanting" an object or a state of affairs at §37 do not necessarily apply to wanting to do something. Say I notice a spot on the wall-paper and get out of my chair. Asked what I am doing I reply "I'm going to see if I can reach it by standing on my toes." Asked why, I reply "I want to, that's all" or "I just had the idea." (Anscombe, 2000, p 91)

While Anscombe thinks that a person cannot intelligibly want just any *object*, she does not rule out the possibility that a person can want to *do* any proposed action. If someone wants "to count blades of grass in various geometrically shaped areas such as park squares and well-trimmed lawns," to use an example that John Rawls (1971, p 432) once imagined, this want is indeed intelligible just as it stands. And while it's also possible for someone to want to count blades of grass for some further reason, this need not be so. On Anscombe's view, *any* type of action can be wanted for no reason. Of course, actions *done* for no reason are not normatively supported in the way that actions performed for reasons are. If I'm doodling for no reason, then this action is hardly normatively supported or justified. Actions are normatively supported by reasons just when they can be rationalized by a desirability characterization.

How does all of this help us think about the Heartless Husband problem, and ultimately with whether Anscombeans can meet the Normative Constraint? We can show that the Heartless Husband has a reason to treat his wife better if doing so would be a part of or means to some other activity he is up to. The activity in question need not be eudaimon-ing. It could be lots of things, such as *getting in shape*, *making his own life less problematic*, or *reducing the amount of yelling in the house*. All of these are desirably characterizable. What's important here is that this activity better not merely be some activity he is doing "for no reason" whatsoever. It just needs to be an activity that can be characterized desirably. *This* would supply him with a reason for treating his wife better.

But suppose, perhaps implausibly, that the Heartless Husband is *not* in fact performing *any* desirably characterizable activity that treating his wife nicely would be a part of or a means to. Treating his wife nicely furthers *no* activity he is up to. Is the Anscombean then at a dead end?

Maybe not. First, perhaps one has a reason to V just in case V-ing *would* connect up with some activity that's desirably characterizable. Suppose it would be healthy for Susan to eat a low-carbohydrate diet. Eating an avocado would be part of eating a low-carbohydrate diet. So, Susan seems to have a reason to eat an avocado, whether or not she is indeed eating a low-carbohydrate diet. The fact that eating a low-carbohydrate diet is healthy counts in favor of eating an avocado. Why does she have a reason for eating an avocado? Because it is part of eating a low-carbohydrate diet. That's her reason. Why is this reason a *good* reason, a reason that counts in favor of eating an avocado? Because eating a low-carbohydrate diet is healthy; it can be desirably characterized. This account marries what's plausible about factualism with the rest of the structure of naïve action theory. By pointing out how some activities are good, this kind of account can meet the Normative Constraint. And by identifying these activities as reasons for their means and parts, this kind of account can meet both the Explanatory Constraint and the Knowledge Constraint.

The most significant problem for *this* version of the Anscombean account concerns whether it meets the Ownership Constraint. Suppose Susan doesn't care even the slightest about her health. She recognizes that eating a low-carbohydrate diet would be healthy, but that does not weigh with her at all. Is it bluff for us to remain steadfast in our claim that she nevertheless has a reason to eat an avocado?

To answer this, we should look at the account favored by Philippa Foot, Anscombe's best-known devotee. Foot weds an Anscombean view of practical reason with an unabashed ethical naturalism. In her book *Natural Goodness* (2001), Foot argues that what counts as good and proper reasoning about what to do depends upon facts about what *kind* of creatures we are. Individual human beings act well when they practically reason in substantive patterns characteristic of humankind. Just as whether you have good eyesight or good sleeping habits depends at least in part upon how human beings characteristically see and sleep, whether you reason well about what to do also depends at least in part upon how human beings characteristically reason. And humans beings characteristically reason in ways that are at least somewhat prudent and beneficent.

Foot's approach suggests a different sort of reply to the challenge posed by the case of the Heartless Husband. Perhaps he has reason to treat his wife more nicely, not because doing so is wanted, nor because it is just plain good or desirable, but because humans beings—of whom he is one—characteristically treat their family at least half-decently. Completely selfish human beings are thankfully anomalous. This places the source of normativity of reasons neither primarily in one's psychology or other individual characteristics, nor in facts completely external and alien to us, but rather in something between: our common humanity. Perhaps this is enough to meet the Ownership Constraint. If successful, we can see how the example of the Heartless Husband (and other anomalous characters) poses no great threat to Foot's Anscombean view.

But there are other impediments Footians face if they aim to meet the Normative Constraint. Human beings may characteristically act in ways both prudent and benevolent, but an honest anthropology will also reveal that we also characteristically act in ways both belligerent and self-destructive. We must take the ugly with the attractive. And so if our common humanity can rationally vindicate acting beneficently, then it can also vindicate acting belligerently. It appears that Footian naturalism, in attempting to show how we have reason to act morally, is also committed to the conclusion that we have reason to act immorally. And this doesn't square with the Normative Constraint, as we would like to understand it. Perhaps human beings really *can* be reasonably vicious.

This is the same sort of problem that we identified with Schroeder's Hypotheticalism. Recall that in attempting to show that everyone has a reason to act morally, Schroeder inadvertently showed that everyone has a reason to act immorally as well. Both Schroeder's and Foot's accounts, then, have the problem of figuring out how we are to weigh reasons for action against one another in a way that yields acceptable conclusions.

Anscombe herself saw this. She (2006, p 147) imagines that someone might ask, "But may not someone be criticizable for pursuing a certain end, thus characterizable as a sort of good of his, where and when it is quite inappropriate for him to do so, or by means inimical to other ends which he ought to have?" She answers, "only if man has a last end which governs all." That is, someone is criticizable for pursuing one good rather than another good only if there is some master end, such as eudaimonia, that directs one to prioritize pursuing the second good over the pursuit of the first. This, she thinks, is not a question that will be settled by a theory of practical reason alone. It is *instead* an ethical question.

CONCLUSION

Foot (1978, p 148) once notably wrote "I am sure that I do not understand the idea of a reason for acting, and I wonder whether anyone else does either." Mysteries indeed remain, but we are not completely in the dark. Reasons for action *explain* and *count in favor* of the actions for which they are reasons, and they *belong* to and are *spontaneously known* by the person whose reasons they are. We have looked at several different ways of understanding how reasons for action can do all these things. None seem perfect. Only factualism and hybrid theories seem to fully meet the Normative Constraint. Only Anscombean and constitutivist views seem to meet the Knowledge Constraint, although there are emerging hybrid theories that aspire to do better (Setiya, 2007). People still disagree over whether it is legitimate to divorce an account of the reasons that explain action from an account of the reasons that count in favor of actions.

We started out with Plato's idea that Reason puts the entire soul in order, doing what is best for itself. It does this by getting all of one's activities aligned with each other, so that one is not fighting against oneself. Now oddly, our various criteria of what counts as a reason seem to struggle against each other—that is, in trying to meet some of the Constraints, we make it more difficult to meet the others. This curious result suggests that we might not be able to fully understand the nature of reasons until we ourselves are fully reasonable, a depressing conclusion I've reached before (Wiland, 2000). Perhaps only the wise can do philosophy well.

NOTES

Chapter One

1 Compare Plato to Descartes, who describes "reason" or "common sense" as the *power* of judging well and of distinguishing the true from the false. See (Descartes, 2006). It's not obvious that a power is the same as a kind of wanting or loving.

2 Such thinkers typically distinguish normative reasons from explanatory reasons, and hold a nonreductive view only of the former. This is an important complication I set aside in the main text for ease of exposition.

Chapter Two

1 Why only "often"? Perhaps Davidson here wanted to allow for reasons that merely explain in the way that other things explain, and are not also reasons *for* action.

2 I thank Eric Marcus and Mark Schroeder for each discussing this idea with me.

3 Thanks to John Brunero for the example.

4 Parfit, 1997 reasonably complains that Williams here seems to assume that reasons-talk is reducible to some other sort of discourse. But why think that reasons *are* reducible in the first place?

Chapter Three

1 It is true that Davidson taught us that a (primary) reason is a belief–desire *pair*. Reflecting on this, one might be tempted to think that

the Davidsonian can be saved from this objection by emphasizing the fact that the paint-drinker lacks a suitable belief, and so lacks a Davidsonian reason at all, which is the result that we hope for. But we must resist this temptation. For the agent presumably believes that by drinking what's in the can, he is thereby drinking a can of paint. Combined with the urge to drink a can of paint, we have exactly what Davidson described as a reason to drink what's in the can. But the man has no more reason to drink what's in the can than he has to drink a can of paint.

2 Schroeder, 2008, pp 92–7 argues that our intuitions about the existence of weak reasons are not very trustworthy.

3 He also argues that we have reasons to act altruistically, even if doing so serves no pre-existing desire. His argument for this claim is significantly more complex, and also more suspect. I thus focus here instead upon his argument for reasons to act prudentially.

4 Actually, the awkward terms of Aristotle's usual English translators.

Chapter Four

1 I say "seem" because Broome, 2008 has a different interpretation of these examples.

2 For more on this, see Wiland, 2003.

3 Thanks to John Brunero for articulating this point.

Chapter Six

1 Velleman, 2000 has repeatedly emphasized that it's also the case that to *suppose* p is to regard p to be true (for a certain purpose), and to *imagine* p is to regard p to be true (again, for a certain purpose). There are a variety of attitudes others than belief that have some connection to the notion of truth. But we think that the connection between truth and belief is in some way tighter or closer than the connection between truth and attitudes like imagining or supposing. How can we express this idea, the idea that what it is to be a belief is connected with the thought that beliefs aim at the truth? It's an interesting question, but even to attempt to answer it adequately here would take us too far afield.

2 The main notable exception is the highly interesting Korsgaard, 2009.

3 There are surely instances of human activity that seem to straddle the line between full-blooded intentional action and mere behavior: driving your car along a familiar route while your mind is wandering, sleepwalking, reflex behavior, compulsions, and so on. Because these can be borderline cases, it is often difficult to know what to say about them. It can even seem appropriate to make Plato's move, ascribing these activities to only *part* of you. But to bring out what's distinctive about action—full-blooded intentional action—and what's distinctive about the way we know what we are doing, we need to limit ourselves to examples that aren't near this border.

4 I set aside here the question of whether and in what way knowledge of one's reasons for belief is, like practical knowledge, spontaneous. That's a very difficult question.

Chapter Seven

1 Actually, we shouldn't just assume that the relevant class here is, or is always, "human beings." Perhaps it is animals, animals with reason, and/or that human beings who live in certain forms of society. For the moment, let's ignore this complication.

2 One interesting difference between Anscombe's view and Thompson's: Anscombe held that an action is intentional just in case the "Why?" question asked about it could be answered in a particular way. By contrast, Thompson argues that an action is intentional just in case it can serve as the *answer* to the "Why?" question. Though different, these proposals are not strictly incompatible: intentional actions might be such that they can serve as a certain kind of answer only if they themselves are explained in a particular sort of way.

3 (Millgram 2009) is to be credited for coining this characterization of Thompson's view.

4 Again, that I was killing the rats in my yard does not mean that I ever killed them. Many of the things that we were once doing never get done.

5 Quinn, 1993; Foot, 2001 argue that if the evil are not ipso facto irrational, we need not worry about rationality. This is an overreaction. If the evil are not ipso facto irrational, then acting

contrary to reason isn't the *only* way to act badly. But it is still one way. (John Brunero pointed this out to me.)

6   To claim that they ordinarily require no further vindication is not to deny that there could be circumstances in which their sense could be questioned. While the question "Why are you eating?" would usually be misplaced, it would be perfectly appropriately asked of a boxer gorging right before the weigh-in ceremony. The fact that such a question is well placed in some circumstance does not establish that it is usually well placed.

7   Of course, there are examples of desirability characterizations besides the suitable and the pleasant. Still, it's interesting that Aristotle latches on to the two types of good prized by the two irrational parts of Plato's tripartite soul: the spirited part of the soul aims at what's honorable or suitable, while the appetitive part aims at what's immediately pleasant.

FURTHER READING

You can find many excellent articles and books cited in the main text. But here I list some additional items for further reading not cited there.

For more on internal and external reasons, see Cohon, 1986; Williams, 1989; Darwall, 1992; McDowell, 1995; Smith, 1995; Millgram, 1996; Sobel, 2001; Finlay, 2009.

For more on the relation between reasons and causes, see Audi, 1986; Collins, 1997; Bittner, 2001; Alvarez, 2009; Setiya, 2011.

For more on the relation between reasons, oughts, and rationality, see Broome, 2000; Wallace, 2001; Broome, 2005; Raz, 2005; Kolodny, 2005; Brunero, 2009; Brunero, 2010.

For more on the wrong-kind-of-reason debate, see Rabinowicz and Rønnow-Rasmussen, 2004; Olson, 2004; Hieronymi, 2005; Rabinowicz and Rønnow-Rasmussen, 2006.

Finally, see the following entries from the *Stanford Encyclopedia of Philosophy*: Finlay and Schroeder, 2008; Millgram, 2008; Ridge, 2008; Wallace, 2008; Lenman, 2010.

BIBLIOGRAPHY

Alvarez, M. (2009), How many kinds of reasons? *Philosophical Explorations*, 12(2), pp. 181–93

Anscombe, G. E. M. (2000), *Intention*, 2nd ed. Harvard University Press: Cambridge, MA

—(2006), *Human Life, Action and Ethics: Essays*, Imprint Academic: Exeter

Audi, R. (1986), Acting for reasons, *Philosophical Review*, 95(4), pp 511–46

Bennett, J F (1989), *Events and Their Names*, Hackett Pub Co Inc: Indiana

Bittner, R. (2001), *Doing Things for Reasons*, Oxford University Press: Oxford

Boyle, M. and Lavin, D. (2010), Goodness and desire. In *Desire, Practical Reason, and the Good*, ed. S Tenenbaum, Oxford University Press: Oxford

Broome, J. (2000), Normative requirements. In *Normativity*, Blackwell: Cambridge

—(2004), Reasons. In *Reason and Value: Essays on the Moral Philosophy of Joseph Raz*, Oxford University Press: Oxford

—(2005), Does rationality give us reasons? *Philosophical Issues*, 15(1), pp. 321–37

—(2008), Reply to Southwood, Kearns and Star, and Cullity, *Ethics*, 119(1), pp. 96–108

Brown, E. (2006), Wishing for fortune, choosing activity: Aristotle on external goods and happiness, *Proceedings of the Boston Area Colloquium in Ancient Philosophy* 22, pp. 221–56

Brunero, J. (2009), Reasons and evidence one ought, *Ethics*, 119(3), pp. 538–45

—(2010), The scope of rational requirements, *Philosophical Quarterly*, 60(238), pp. 28–49

Clark, P. (2001), Velleman's autonomism, *Ethics*, 111(3), pp. 580–93

Cohon, R. (1986), Are external reasons impossible? *Ethics*, 96(3), pp. 545–56

Collins, A. W. (1997), The psychological reality of reasons. *Ratio*, 10(2), pp. 108–23

Dancy, J. (1995), Why there is really no such thing as the theory of motivation, *Proceedings of the Aristotelian Society*, 95, pp. 1–18

—(2003), *Practical Reality*, Oxford University Press: Oxford

—(2006), What do reasons do? in (eds) T. Horgan and M. Timmons, *Metaethics After Moore*, Oxford University Press, Oxford: Oxford, pp. 95–113

Darwall, S. L. (1992), Internalism and agency. *Philosophical Perspectives*, 6, pp. 155–74

Davidson, D. (1963), Actions, reasons, and causes. *Journal of Philosophy*, 60, pp 685–99

Davidson, D. (1986), A coherence theory of truth and knowledge, in ed. E LePore, *Truth and Interpretation: Perspectives on the Philosophy of Donald Davidson*. Basil Blackwell: Oxford, pp. 307–19

Descartes, R. (2006), *A Discourse on the Method of Correctly Conducting One's Reason and Seeking Truth in the Sciences*, Oxford University Press: Oxford

Enoch, D. (2006), Agency, shmagency: why normativity won't come from what is constitutive of action, *Philosophical Review*, 115(2), pp. 169–98

Epicurus Inwood, B. and Gerson, L. P. (1994), *The Epicurus Reader: Selected Writings and Testimonia*, Hackett Pub Co: Indianapolis

Finlay, S. (2009), The obscurity of internal reasons. *Philosophers' Imprint*, 9(7), pp. 1–22

Finlay, S. and Schroeder, M. (2008), Reasons for action: internal vs. external. In ed. E Zalta, *Stanford Encyclopedia of Philosophy*.

Foot, P. (1978), *Virtues and Vices and Other Essays in Moral Philosophy*, Basil Blackwell: Oxford

Foot, P. (2001): *Natural Goodness*, Oxford University Press: Oxford

Ford, A. (Unpublished), What is Done: A Theory of Action and Practical Knowledge.

Garrard, E. and McNaughton, D. (1998), Mapping moral motivation. *Ethical Theory and Moral Practice*, 1(1), pp. 45–59

Heuer, U. (2004), Reasons for actions and desires. *Philosophical Studies*, 121(1), pp 43–63

Hieronymi, P. (2005), The wrong kind of reason. *Journal of Philosophy*, 102(9), pp 437–57

Hobbes, T. (1991), *Leviathan*, ed. R. Tuck, Cambridge University Press: Cambridge

Hume, D. (1984), *A Treatise of Human Nature*, Penguin Books: London

—(1998), *An Enquiry Concerning the Principles of Morals*, ed. T L Beauchamp, Oxford University Press: Oxford

Kearns, S. and Star, D. (2008), Reasons: explanations or evidence? *Ethics*, 119(1), pp. 31–56

—(2009), Reasons as evidence. *Oxford Studies in Metaethics*, 4, pp. 215–42

Kolodny, N. (2005), Why be rational? *Mind*, 114(455), pp. 509–63

Korsgaard, C (1986) Skepticism about practical reason. *The Journal of Philosophy*, 83(1), pp. 5–25

—(1996), *The Sources of Normativity*, Cambridge University Press: Cambridge

—(1997), The normativity of instrumental reason. In (eds) G Cullity and B Gaut, *Ethics and Practical Reason*, Clarendon Press: Oxford

—(2008), *The Constitution of Agency: Essays on Practical Reason and Moral Psychology*, Oxford University Press: Oxford

—(2009), *Self-Constitution: Agency, Identity, and Integrity*, Oxford University Press: Oxford

Lavin, D. (2004), Practical reason and the possibility of error, *Ethics*, 114(3), pp. 424–57

Lenman, J. (2010), Reasons for action: justification vs. explanation. In *Stanford Encyclopedia of Philosophy*

McDowell, J. (1979), Virtue and reason. *The Monist*, 62(3).

—(1995), Might there be external reasons? In (eds) J. E. J. Altham and R Harrison, *World, Mind and Ethics: Essays on the Ethical Philosophy of Bernard Williams*, Cambridge University Press: Cambridge

Millgram, E. (1996), Williams' argument against external reasons, *Noûs*, 30(2), pp. 197–220

—(2008), Practical reason and the structure of actions. In *Stanford Encyclopedia of Philosophy*

—(2009), Review of Life and Action, *Analysis*, 69(3), pp. 557–64

Nagel, T. (1971), *The Possibility of Altruism*, Oxford University Press: Oxford

Norman, R. (2001), Practical reasons and the redundancy of motives, *Ethical Theory and Moral Practice*, 4(1), pp. 3–22

Olson, J. (2004), Buck-passing and the wrong kind of reasons, *Philosophical Quarterly*, 54(215), pp. 295–300

Parfit, D. (1997), Reasons and motivation, *Aristotelian Society Supplementary Volume*, 71(1), pp. 99–130

—(2011), *On What Matters*, Oxford University Press: Oxford

Quinn, W (1993), Putting Rationality in its Place. In (eds) R. G. Frey and C. Morris, *Value, Welfare, and Morality*, Cambridge University Press: Cambridge

Rabinowicz, W. and Rønnow-Rasmussen, T. (2004), The strike of the demon: on fitting pro-attitudes and value. *Ethics*, 114(3), pp. 391–423

—(2006), Buck-passing and the right kind of reasons. *Philosophical Quarterly*, 56(222), pp. 114–20

Rawls, J. (1971), *A Theory of Justice*, Harvard University Press: Cambridge, MA

Raz, J. (1999), *Engaging Reason: On the Theory of Value and Action*, Oxford University Press: Oxford

Raz, J. (2005), The Myth of Instrumental Rationality, *Journal of Ethics and Social Philosophy*, 1(1), pp. 1–28

Ridge, M. (2008), Reasons for Action: Agent-Neutral vs. Agent-Relative. In *The Stanford Encyclopedia of Philosophy*

Scanlon, T. M. (2000), *What We Owe to Each Other*, Belknap Press of Harvard University Press

Schroeder, M. (2008), *Slaves of the Passions*, Oxford University Press: Oxford

Setiya, K. (2007), *Reasons without Rationalism*, Princeton University Press: Princeton

—(2011), Reasons and Causes, *European Journal of Philosophy*, 19(1), pp. 129–57

Smith, M. (1987), The Humean Theory of Motivation. *Mind*, 96(381), pp. 36–61

—(1994), *The Moral Problem*, Basil Blackwell. Oxford

—(1995), Internal reasons, *Philosophy and Phenomenological Research*, 55(1), pp 109–31

Sobel, D. (2001), Explanation, internalism, and reasons for action. *Social Philosophy and Policy*, 18(2), pp. 218–

Thompson, M. (2008), *Life and Action: Elementary Structures of Practice and Practical Thought*, Harvard University Press: Cambridge, MA

—(2011), Anscombe's intention and practical knowledge. In (eds) A Ford, J. Hornsby, and F. Stoutland, *Essays on Anscombe's Intention*, Harvard University Press: Cambridge, MA

Velleman, J. D. (2000), *The Possibility of Practical Reason*, Oxford University Press: Oxford

Vogler, C. A. (2002), *Reasonably Vicious*, Harvard University Press: Cambridge, MA

Wallace, R. J. (2001), Normativity, commitment, and instrumental reason. *Philosophers' Imprint*, 1(3), pp. 1–19

—(2008), Practical reason. In *Stanford Encyclopedia of Philosophy*

Watson, G. (1975), Free Agency, *The Journal of Philosophy*, 72(8), pp. 205–20

Wiland, E. (2000), Good advice and rational action, *Philosophy and Phenomenological Research*, 60(3), pp. 561–9

—(2003), Psychologism, practical reason and the possibility of error, *Philosophical Quarterly*, 53(210), pp. 68–78

Williams, B. (1981), Internal and external reasons. In ed B Williams, *Moral Luck*, Cambridge University Press: Cambridge, pp. 101–13

—(1989), Internal reasons and the obscurity of blame. In ed. B Williams, *Making Sense of Humanity*, Cambridge University Press, Cambridge: pp. 35–45

Winters, B. (1979), Hume on reason. *Hume Studies*, 5(1), pp. 20–35

Woods, M. (1972), Reasons for Action and Desires, *Aristotelian Society Supplementary Volume*, 46, pp. 189–201

INDEX